Pillsbury

easy pie

MW01156288

140 simple recipes **+** 1 readymade pie crust

= *sweet success*

WILEY

Wiley Publishing, Inc.

General Mills

Editorial Director: Jeff Nowak

Publishing Manager: Christine Gray

Cookbook Manager and Editor:
Lois Tlusty

Recipe Development and Testing:
Pillsbury Kitchens

Photography: General Mills
Photography Studios and Image
Library

Photographer: Val Bourassa

Food Stylist: Nancy Johnson

Wiley Publishing, Inc.

Publisher: Natalie Chapman

Associate Publisher: Jessica Goodman

Executive Editor: Anne Ficklen

Editor: Adam Kowit

Editorial Assistant: Cecily McAndrews

Production: Amy Zarkos and Kristi
Hart

Cover Design: Suzanne Sunwoo

Art Director and Interior Design:
Tai Blanche

Layout: Indy Composition Services

Photography Art Direction:
Chris Everett/See Design, Inc.

Prop Stylist: Michele Joy

Manufacturing Manager: Kevin Watt

This book is printed on acid-free paper. ∞

For general information on our other products and services or for technical support, please contact our Customer Care Department within the United States at (877) 762-2974, outside the United States at (317) 572-3993 or fax (317) 572-4002.

Wiley also publishes its books in a variety of electronic formats. Some content that appears in print may not be available in electronic books. For more information about Wiley products, visit our web site at www.wiley.com.

Library of Congress Cataloging-in-Publication Data:

Pillsbury easy as pie.
   p. cm.
   Includes index.
   ISBN 978-0-470-48553-8 (cloth)
   1. Pies. 2. Brand name products.
   TX773.P5735 2010
   641.8'652—dc22

                       2009005652

Manufactured in China

10 9 8 7 6 5 4 3 2 1

Cover photo: Orchard Medley Pie (page 34)

Home of the Pillsbury Bake-Off® Contest

Pillsbury

Our recipes have been tested in the Pillsbury Kitchens and meet our standards of easy preparation, reliability and great taste.

For more great recipes, visit pillsbury.com

Dear Friends,

Easy as pie, a well-known phrase that can be traced back to 1887, means "very easy."

Pillsbury Easy as Pie cookbook does just that—makes pie baking "very easy" with the help of Pillsbury® refrigerated pie crust. Making a perfect pie crust can be a challenge. Starting with refrigerated pie crust ensures you'll get a tender flaky crust every time. Then get ready for rave reviews (it's up to you whether to share your secret for perfect pie crust made easy).

Scrumptious homemade pies and tarts make any occasion extra-special. Enjoy the fall harvest with a juicy Cinnamon Apple Crostata, page 20, or celebrate the holidays with a traditional Pumpkin Pie, page 144. Surprise your family by serving a creamy French Silk Chocolate Pie, page 70, just to say "I love you!"

Pies aren't just for dessert. Check out the Savory Pies and Quiches chapter, and you're sure to find a pie or quiche for brunch, a quick dinner or any time you're having people over. After all, who can resist a warm, mouthwatering pie fresh from the oven?

Let's bake a pie and make tonight special!

Warmly,

Lois Tlusty

Pillsbury Editor

Caramel Apple Pie, page 14

Cranberry Mousse Mini Tarts, page 126

Chocolate-Strawberry Pie, page 74

Chocolate-Strawberry Pie, page 74

contents

Start with the Right Pie Pan

Refrigerated pie crusts are designed for 8-inch or 9-inch pie pans and 10-inch tart pans.

Use the size pan that is called for in the recipes. If the pan is too small, there will be too much filling—a two-crust pie could bubble over in the oven during baking. A pan too large will result in a low-volume pie.

A glass pie plate or dull-metal pie pan is best because the crust bakes evenly to a golden brown and is tender and flaky. A shiny or disposable aluminum pan reflects heat and prevents the crust from browning, and results in an underbaked bottom crust. A dark pan absorbs heat, which causes too much browning.

Nonstick pie pans can cause an unfilled one-crust pie to shrink excessively during baking because the crust can't cling to the side of the pan. To hold the crust in place, be sure the decorative edge (fluted edge) extends over the edge of the pan and is firmly pressed under the edge. In addition, lining the unbaked crust with foil and filling it with raw rice or beans helps to prevent shrinkage.

Handle Pie Crust Correctly

Let refrigerated crusts stand at room temperature for 15 minutes, or microwave one pouch on Defrost for 10 to 20 seconds before unrolling. If crusts are frozen, remove frozen crusts from box and let stand at room temperature 60 to 90 minutes before unrolling. Slowly and gently unroll in the pie plate.

To keep the crust from pulling from the side of the pie plate during baking, press it firmly against the side and bottom of the pie plate. Be sure not to stretch the crust.

Handling Pie Crust

Unroll the crust slowly and gently into the plate

Gently press the crust against the side of the pie plate.

Baking Unfilled Pie Crust

To prevent bubbles from forming in an unfilled one-crust pie, generously prick the side and bottom of the crust with a fork before baking. If bubbles do form, press them down gently with the back of a wooden spoon. Continue baking until the crust is done.

Prick the crust generously with a fork.

Cover the edge of the crust with foil.

Keep the baked edge from getting too brown by covering it with foil after the first 15 minutes of baking or as directed in the recipe. Use a 12-inch square of foil; cut out a 7-inch circle from the center, and gently fold the foil "ring" around the crust's edge. Or use strips of foil on the edge of the crust. Be careful—the pie will be hot if you add the foil during baking.

Crumb Crusts

For some pudding-type pies and ice cream pies, you may want to try a crumb crust instead of the pastry crust. They're easy to make. Here are three basic crumb crusts.

CRUST	BUTTER OR MARGARINE	CRUMBS	SUGAR
Graham Cracker	⅓ cup	1½ cups (about 24 squares, finely crushed)	3 tablespoons
Chocolate Cookie	¼ cup	1½ cups (about 30 chocolate cookies, finely crushed)	Omit
Vanilla Cookie	¼ cup	1½ cups (about 38 vanilla cookies, finely crushed)	Omit

1 Heat oven to 400°F. Place the butter in a small microwavable bowl; cover with a microwavable paper towel. Microwave on High 30 to 50 seconds or until melted. Place crumbs and sugar in medium bowl; pour butter over crumb mixture. Toss until well mixed.

2 Reserve 3 tablespoons crumb mixture for sprinkling on top of pie if desired. Using fingers, press remaining mixture firmly against the bottom and side of ungreased 9-inch glass pie plate. Bake about 10 minutes or until light brown. Cool completely on cooling rack, about 15 minutes. Fill crust as directed in pie recipe.

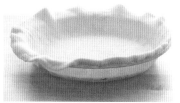

Forming Stand-up Rim

Fold edge under and press to seal.

Forming Scalloped Edge

Push dough with index finger toward outside.

Forming Rope Edge

Pinch crust between thumb and knuckle of index finger.

Creative Fun Edges

The fluted edge of a pie not only adds a decorative touch, but also helps to prevent the filling from bubbling over. Here are three fluted edges that are easy and fun.

FORKED OR HERRINGBONE EDGE

Trim the crust even with the edge of the pan. Dip the fork tines in flour, and then press them diagonally onto the edge without pressing through the dough. Rotate the tines 90 degrees, and press them next to the first set of marks. Continue around the edge, rotating the tines back and forth. (See page 159 for example.)

SCALLOPED AND ROPE EDGES

A stand-up rim is used before fluting a scalloped or rope edge. Fold overhanging crust under itself and even with plate edge, pressing to seal and form a stand-up rim (see photo). Press rim together to make it even thickness.

Scalloped Edge: Trim the crust even with the edge of the pan and form a stand-up rim. Place your left thumb and index finger about 1 inch apart on the outside of the raised edge. With your right forefinger, push the dough toward the outside to form a scalloped wave (see photo).

Rope Edge: Fold and roll overhanging crust under edge of bottom crust; press to seal. Form a stand-up rim of even thickness. Place side of your thumb on the crust rim at an angle. Pinch crust by pressing the knuckle of your index finger down into crust toward thumb (see photo).

Lattice Top Crusts

A lattice crust adds a nice touch to any two-crust pie because the bubbly filling can peek through. Thankfully, they're not nearly as hard to make as they look. The first method below is quicker, while the second is more traditional. Whichever one you choose, they're both beautiful and tasty.

Easy Lattice Top: Prepare crust for a two-crust pie, leaving ½ inch of the bottom crust extending beyond the edge of the pan. Place the filling in the crust-lined pan. Cut the remaining crust into about ½-inch-wide strips. Place strips about ½ inch apart on the filling. Place the remaining strips about ½ inch apart across the first row (see page 159 for an example of how this looks). Trim the strips evenly with the edge of the extended crust. Fold the edge up, forming a high stand-up rim edge; flute the edge as desired. A lattice-topped fruit pie is more likely to bubble over than a two-crust pie, so the higher rim is necessary.

Classic Lattice Top: Make the same as the Easy Lattice Top—except after placing the strips about ½ inch apart on the filling, fold back alternating strips before adding the cross-strips.

Q&A: Refrigerated Pie Crust

Q How long can I store an unopened box of pie crusts?

A For best quality, use refrigerated pie crusts before the "use-by" date on the package.

Q Can I freeze unbaked pie crusts?

A Yes, pie crusts may be frozen up to two months if placed in the freezer before the "use-by" date.

Q Can I defrost frozen, unbaked crusts in the microwave?

A No, because the uneven heat of a microwave may melt some parts of the crust.

Q Can I soften refrigerated crusts in the microwave?

A Yes. Microwave each refrigerated crust on Defrost for 10 to 20 seconds. Do not microwave frozen crusts.

Freezing Pies

UNBAKED PIES

Fruit pies can be frozen before baking.

1 Brush the bottom crust with egg white before adding the filling to prevent sogginess.

2 Add the fruit filling. Do not slit the top crust before placing over the filling. Seal and flute the edge as desired.

3 Cover the pie with an inverted paper plate, wrap it tightly and freeze it up to three months.

To bake a frozen pie:

1 Do not thaw the pie.

2 Unwrap the pie, and cut slits in the top crust.

3 Bake the pie at 425°F for 15 minutes. Reduce the temperature to 375°F, and bake 30 to 45 minutes or until center is bubbly.

BAKED PIES

Baked pumpkin, pecan and fruit pies can be frozen. Do not freeze custard or cream pies or pies with meringue toppings because they break down and become watery.

1 After baking the pie, cool it completely. Wrap it tightly and freeze up to four months.

2 To thaw, unwrap the pie and heat at 325°F for 45 minutes or until the center is warm.

✳ ✳ ✳ storing baked pies

A fruit pie can be stored at room temperature up to two days. All pies containing eggs, dairy products or meat (including custard or cream pies, quiches and main-dish pies) must be stored in the refrigerator for no more than two days. Be sure to store as directed in the recipe.

✳ cutting pies ✳ ✳ ✳ ✳ ✳ ✳ ✳

Cut cooled pies with a sharp, thin-bladed knife. For meringue or ice cream pies, dip the knife in warm water and wipe clean before cutting.

fruit and berry harvest

Cinnamon Apple Crostata, page 20

perfect apple pie

Prep Time: 35 Minutes ✳ Start to Finish: 3 Hours 20 Minutes ✳ 8 servings

CRUST

1 box (15 oz) Pillsbury®
   refrigerated pie crusts,
   softened as directed on box

FILLING*

6 cups thinly sliced peeled
   apples (6 medium)

¾ cup sugar

2 tablespoons all-purpose
   flour

¾ teaspoon ground cinnamon

¼ teaspoon salt

⅛ teaspoon ground nutmeg

1 tablespoon lemon juice

1 Heat oven to 425°F. Make pie crusts as directed on box for Two-Crust Pie, using 9-inch glass pie plate.

2 In large bowl, gently mix filling ingredients; spoon into pastry-lined pie plate. Top with second crust; seal edge and flute. Cut slits or shapes in several places in top crust. Cover edge with foil to prevent excessive browning.

3 Bake 40 to 45 minutes or until apples are tender and crust is golden brown, removing foil during last 15 minutes of baking. Cool on cooling rack at least 2 hours before serving.

*Two cans (21 oz each) apple pie filling can be substituted for the fresh apple filling.

High Altitude (3500–6500 ft): No change.

1 Serving: Calories 400; Total Fat 18g (Saturated Fat 4.5g; Trans Fat 3g); Cholesterol 0mg; Sodium 370mg; Total Carbohydrate 57g (Dietary Fiber 3g) **Exchanges:** 1 Starch, 3 Other Carbohydrate, 3½ Fat **Carbohydrate Choices:** 4

Pie Tip Tart apples, such as Granny Smith, McIntosh or Pippin, make the most flavorful pies.

apple praline pie

Prep Time: 30 Minutes * Start to Finish: 4 Hours 30 Minutes * 8 servings

CRUST
1 box (15 oz) Pillsbury refrigerated pie crusts, softened as directed on box

FILLING*
6 cups thinly sliced peeled apples (6 medium)

¾ cup granulated sugar

¼ cup all-purpose flour

1 teaspoon ground cinnamon

¼ teaspoon salt

1 tablespoon butter or margarine

TOPPING
¼ cup butter or margarine

½ cup packed brown sugar

2 tablespoons half-and-half or milk

½ cup chopped pecans

1 Heat oven to 350°F. Make pie crusts as directed on box for Two-Crust Pie, using 9-inch glass pie plate.

2 In large bowl, mix apples, granulated sugar, flour, cinnamon and salt; toss lightly. Spoon mixture into crust-lined pie plate. Dot with 1 tablespoon butter. Top with second crust; seal edge and flute. Cut slits or shapes in several places in top crust.

3 Bake 50 to 55 minutes or until apples are tender and crust is golden brown. Cover crust edge with foil after 15 to 20 minutes of bake time to prevent excessive browning.

4 In 1-quart saucepan, melt ¼ cup butter; stir in brown sugar and half-and-half. Slowly heat to boiling; remove from heat. Stir in pecans; spread over top of pie. Place pie on cookie sheet.

5 Bake about 5 minutes longer or until topping bubbles. Cool on cooling rack at least 3 hours before serving.

*Two cans (21 oz each) apple pie filling can be substituted for the fresh apple filling.

High Altitude (3500–6500 ft): Heat oven to 375°F. In step 3, bake 55 to 60 minutes.

1 Serving: Calories 540; Total Fat 27g (Saturated Fat 10g; Trans Fat 0g); Cholesterol 30mg; Sodium 350mg; Total Carbohydrate 73g (Dietary Fiber 2g) **Exchanges:** ½ Starch, ½ Fruit, 4 Other Carbohydrate, 5 Fat **Carbohydrate Choices:** 5

Pie Tip The crunchy topping on this apple pie combines the noted ingredients of pralines, a well-known New Orleans candy made of pecans and brown sugar. The topping is best when made with butter because it resembles the rich flavor of the praline candies.

caramel apple pie

Prep Time: 20 Minutes ✳ Start to Finish: 2 Hours 5 Minutes ✳ 8 servings

CRUST
1 box (15 oz) Pillsbury refrigerated pie crusts, softened as directed on box

¼ cup finely chopped pecans

FILLING*
¾ cup sugar

2 tablespoons all-purpose flour

1 teaspoon ground cinnamon

⅛ teaspoon ground nutmeg

1 tablespoon lemon juice

6 cups sliced peeled apples (6 medium)

TOPPING
⅓ cup caramel topping

¼ cup chopped pecans

SERVE WITH, IF DESIRED
Vanilla ice cream

Additional caramel topping

Additional chopped pecans

1 Heat oven to 425°F. Make pie crusts as directed on box for Two-Crust Pie, using 9-inch glass pie plate. Sprinkle ¼ cup finely chopped pecans in bottom of crust-lined pie plate.

2 In large bowl, mix sugar, flour, cinnamon and nutmeg. Gently stir in lemon juice and apples. Spoon into crust-lined pie plate. Top with second crust; seal edge and flute. Cut slits or shapes in several places in top crust. If desired, brush crust with water; sprinkle lightly with sugar.

3 Bake 35 to 45 minutes or until apples are tender and crust is golden brown. After 15 to 20 minutes of bake time, cover crust edge with foil to prevent excessive browning. Immediately after removing pie from oven, drizzle with ⅓ cup caramel topping; sprinkle with ¼ cup chopped pecans. Cool on cooling rack at least 1 hour before serving.

4 Serve warm pie with ice cream; drizzle with caramel topping and sprinkle with pecans.

✶Two cans (21 oz each) apple pie filling can be substituted for the fresh apple filling.

High Altitude (3500–6500 ft): Before baking, cover crust edge with foil to prevent excessive browning; remove foil during last 5 minutes of baking.

1 Serving: Calories 440; Total Fat 19g (Saturated Fat 5g; Trans Fat 0g); Cholesterol 10mg; Sodium 270mg; Total Carbohydrate 67g (Dietary Fiber 2g) **Exchanges:** 1 Starch, 3½ Other Carbohydrate, 3½ Fat **Carbohydrate Choices:** 4½

 Pie Tip Chopped walnuts can be used instead of the pecans for a different nutty taste. If you have apple pie spice on hand, use 1¼ teaspoons instead of the cinnamon and nutmeg.

sour cream–apple pie

Prep Time: 30 Minutes ✳ Start to Finish: 3 Hours 40 Minutes ✳ 8 servings

CRUST

1 Pillsbury refrigerated pie crust (from 15-oz box), softened as directed on box

FILLING

1¼ cups sour cream

¾ cup granulated sugar

¼ cup all-purpose flour

¼ teaspoon salt

2 teaspoons vanilla

1 egg

6 cups ¼-inch slices peeled baking apples (6 medium)

STREUSEL

½ cup all-purpose flour

½ cup chopped walnuts

¼ cup granulated sugar

¼ cup packed light brown sugar

½ teaspoon ground cinnamon

Dash salt

3 tablespoons cold butter or margarine

1 Heat oven to 400°F. Place pie crust in 9-inch glass pie plate as directed on box for One-Crust Filled Pie.

2 In large bowl, beat sour cream, granulated sugar, flour, salt, vanilla and egg with whisk until well blended; gently stir in apples until evenly coated. Pour into crust-lined pie plate. Cover crust edge with foil to prevent excessive browning.

3 Bake 15 minutes. Reduce oven temperature to 350°F. Bake 30 minutes longer.

4 Meanwhile, in medium bowl, mix all streusel ingredients except butter. Cut in butter, using pastry blender (or fork or pulling 2 table knives through mixture in opposite directions), until mixture looks like coarse crumbs; refrigerate until ready to use.

5 Remove foil from crust. Sprinkle streusel over pie. Bake 20 to 25 minutes longer or until streusel is golden brown. Cool completely on cooling rack, about 2 hours. Cover and refrigerate any remaining pie.

High Altitude (3500–6500 ft): In step 5, bake 25 to 30 minutes.

1 Serving: Calories 500; Total Fat 24g (Saturated Fat 10g; Trans Fat 0g); Cholesterol 65mg; Sodium 260mg; Total Carbohydrate 67g (Dietary Fiber 2g) **Exchanges:** 1 Starch, 3½ Other Carbohydrate, 4½ Fat **Carbohydrate Choices:** 4½

apple–cream cheese pie

Prep Time: 35 Minutes ✳ Start to Finish: 2 Hours 30 Minutes ✳ 8 servings

CRUST

1 Pillsbury refrigerated pie crust (from 15-oz box), softened as directed on box

STREUSEL

¾ cup packed brown sugar

½ cup all-purpose flour

½ cup old-fashioned or quick-cooking oats

¾ teaspoon apple pie spice

⅓ cup butter or margarine

APPLE LAYER

3 cups thinly sliced peeled apples (3 medium)

⅓ cup granulated sugar

3 tablespoons all-purpose flour

1 teaspoon apple pie spice

CREAM CHEESE LAYER

1 package (8 oz) cream cheese, softened

¼ cup granulated sugar

1 egg

¼ teaspoon vanilla

1 Heat oven to 450°F. Place pie crust in 9-inch glass pie plate as directed on box for One-Crust Baked Shell—except do not prick crust. Bake 9 to 11 minutes or until light brown. If crust puffs in center, flatten gently with back of wooden spoon. Reduce oven temperature to 350°F.

2 Meanwhile, in small bowl, stir together all streusel ingredients except butter. Cut in butter, using pastry blender (or fork or pulling 2 table knives through mixture in opposite directions) until mixture looks like coarse crumbs. Set aside. In large bowl, gently mix apple layer ingredients; set aside.

3 In small bowl, beat cream cheese and ¼ cup granulated sugar with electric mixer on low speed until well blended. Add egg and vanilla; beat well. Spread in crust-lined pie plate. Spoon apple mixture evenly over cream cheese layer; sprinkle with streusel.

4 Bake at 350°F 50 to 60 minutes or until apples are tender and streusel is golden brown. If necessary, cover pie loosely with foil during last 10 to 15 minutes of baking to prevent excessive browning. Cool on cooling rack at least 1 hour before serving. Cover and refrigerate any remaining pie.

High Altitude (3500–6500 ft): No change.

1 Serving: Calories 510; Total Fat 26g (Saturated Fat 14g; Trans Fat 0.5g); Cholesterol 80mg; Sodium 260mg; Total Carbohydrate 66g (Dietary Fiber 1g) **Exchanges:** 1 Starch, 3½ Other Carbohydrate, 5 Fat **Carbohydrate Choices:** 4½

Pie Tip If you don't have apple pie spice, you can use the same amount of pumpkin pie spice. Or if you like, you can make your own 1¾-teaspoon spice blend by mixing 1 teaspoon ground cinnamon and ¼ teaspoon each ground ginger, ground allspice and ground nutmeg.

apple-blueberry pie with strawberry sauce

Prep Time: 30 Minutes * Start to Finish: 3 Hours 30 Minutes * 8 servings

CRUST

1 box (15 oz) Pillsbury refrigerated pie crusts, softened as directed on box

FILLING

5 cups thinly sliced peeled apples (5 medium)

2 cups fresh or frozen (thawed) blueberries

1 cup sugar

½ teaspoon ground cinnamon

3 tablespoons quick-cooking tapioca

2 tablespoons butter or margarine

1 egg

1 teaspoon water

SAUCE

2 cups fresh strawberries

½ cup sugar

1 tablespoon sweet Marsala wine or water

1 tablespoon cornstarch

2 tablespoons water

½ cup whipping cream

1 Heat oven to 400°F. Make pie crusts as directed on box for Two-Crust Pie, using 9-inch glass pie plate.

2 In large bowl, stir together apples, blueberries, 1 cup sugar, the cinnamon and tapioca; let stand 15 minutes. Spoon filling into crust-lined pie plate. Dot with butter. Top with second crust; seal edge and flute. Cut slits or shapes in several places in top crust. Stir together egg and 1 teaspoon water; brush on top of crust.

3 Bake 15 minutes. Cover crust edge with foil. Reduce oven temperature to 350°F. Bake 40 to 45 minutes longer or until apples are tender. Cool on cooling rack at least 2 hours.

4 Meanwhile, crush enough strawberries to measure ⅓ cup. In 1-quart saucepan, mix crushed strawberries, ½ cup sugar and the wine. Heat to boiling over medium heat. Dissolve cornstarch in 2 tablespoons water; stir into strawberry mixture. Boil and stir 2 minutes. Remove from heat; cool to room temperature. Stir in whipping cream. Slice remaining strawberries; stir into sauce. Refrigerate sauce until serving time. Serve sauce with pie.

High Altitude (3500–6500 ft): In step 3, increase first bake time to 20 minutes.

1 Serving: Calories 550; Total Fat 22g (Saturated Fat 10g; Trans Fat 0g); Cholesterol 60mg; Sodium 250mg; Total Carbohydrate 85g (Dietary Fiber 2g) **Exchanges:** ½ Starch, 1 Fruit, 4 Other Carbohydrate, 4½ Fat **Carbohydrate Choices:** 5½

Pie Tip The sweetness of apples varies due to the variety of apple you use. If using a very sweet variety of apple, you may want to decrease the sugar in the filling to ¾ cup.

cinnamon apple crostata

Prep Time: 20 Minutes ✴ Start to Finish: 1 Hour 5 Minutes ✴ 8 servings

CRUST
1 Pillsbury refrigerated pie crust (from 15-oz box), softened as directed on box

FILLING
½ cup sugar

4 teaspoons cornstarch

2 teaspoons ground cinnamon

4 cups thinly sliced peeled apples (4 medium)

1 teaspoon sugar

2 tablespoons chopped pecans or walnuts

SERVE WITH, IF DESIRED
Whipped cream or ice cream

1 Heat oven to 450°F. On ungreased cookie sheet, unroll pie crust.

2 In medium bowl, mix ½ cup sugar, the cornstarch and cinnamon. Gently stir in apples until evenly coated. Spoon filling onto center of crust, spreading to within 2 inches of edge. Carefully fold 2-inch crust edge over filling, pleating crust slightly as necessary. Brush crust edge with water; sprinkle with 1 teaspoon sugar.

3 Bake about 15 minutes or until crust is golden brown. Sprinkle pecans over filling. Bake 5 to 15 minutes longer or until apples are tender. Cool on cooling rack 15 minutes. Cut into wedges, serve warm with whipped cream.

High Altitude (3500–6500 ft): No change.

1 Serving: Calories 220; Total Fat 8g (Saturated Fat 2.5g; Trans Fat 0g); Cholesterol 0mg; Sodium 110mg; Total Carbohydrate 35g (Dietary Fiber 1g) **Exchanges:** 2½ Other Carbohydrate, 1½ Fat **Carbohydrate Choices:** 2

See photo on page 11.

apple tart with cider-bourbon sauce

Prep Time: 25 Minutes ✳ Start to Finish: 1 Hour 45 Minutes ✳ 8 servings

CRUST
1 Pillsbury refrigerated pie
   crust (from 15-oz box),
   softened as directed on box

FILLING
½ cup packed brown sugar

2 tablespoons finely chopped
   crystallized ginger

2 tablespoons cornstarch

1 teaspoon ground cinnamon

4 cups thinly sliced peeled
   cooking apples (4 medium)

SAUCE
1¼ cups apple cider

2 tablespoons butter or
   margarine

2 tablespoons packed brown
   sugar

1 tablespoon cornstarch

2 tablespoons bourbon or
   water

1 Place cookie sheet in oven on middle rack. Heat oven to 450°F. Place pie crust in 9-inch tart pan with removable bottom as directed on box for One-Crust Filled Pie. Bake on preheated cookie sheet 7 minutes.

2 Meanwhile, in large bowl, mix ½ cup brown sugar, the ginger, 2 tablespoons cornstarch and the cinnamon until blended. Gently stir in apples until evenly coated.

3 In crust-lined pan, arrange apples in concentric circles, overlapping slices and using all of apples, beginning at outside edge and working toward center.

4 Cover top of tart with foil; place on preheated cookie sheet. Bake 40 minutes. Remove foil; bake 8 to 10 minutes longer or until apples are tender and crust is golden brown. Place tart pan on cooling rack; cool 30 minutes while making sauce.

5 Meanwhile, in 1-quart saucepan, heat cider to boiling over high heat. Boil 4 to 6 minutes, stirring occasionally, until reduced to 1 cup. Stir in butter and 2 tablespoons brown sugar; continue boiling 2 minutes, stirring occasionally. In small bowl, stir 1 tablespoon cornstarch into bourbon until dissolved. Stir bourbon mixture into sauce; boil 1 minute, stirring constantly. To remove tart from sides of pan, place the pan on a wide, short can and pull down the side of the pan (see page 80). If necessary, use a thin-bladed knife to loosen crust from the side of the pan. Serve tart with warm sauce.

High Altitude (3500–6500 ft): Heat oven to 425°F. Cut apples into very thin slices. In step 4, bake covered on cookie sheet 45 minutes. Remove foil; bake 8 to 10 minutes longer.

1 Serving: Calories 280; Total Fat 10g (Saturated Fat 4.5g; Trans Fat 0g); Cholesterol 10mg; Sodium 140mg; Total Carbohydrate 46g (Dietary Fiber 1g) **Exchanges:** 3 Other Carbohydrate, 2 Fat **Carbohydrate Choices:** 3

Pie Tip Be careful not to stretch the pie crust dough when fitting it into the tart pan. Stretching the dough will cause the crust to shrink during baking.

apple pie foldover

Prep Time: 25 Minutes ✳ Start to Finish: 1 Hour 15 Minutes ✳ 4 servings

FILLING

1½ cups thinly sliced peeled apples (1½ medium)

¼ cup packed brown sugar

1 tablespoon water

1 teaspoon lemon juice

1 tablespoon all-purpose flour

1 tablespoon granulated sugar

¼ teaspoon salt

1 tablespoon butter or margarine

½ teaspoon vanilla

CRUST

1 Pillsbury refrigerated pie crust (from 15-oz box), softened as directed on box

1 egg

1 tablespoon water

1 teaspoon granulated sugar

⅛ teaspoon ground cinnamon

1 In 2-quart saucepan, mix apples, brown sugar, 1 tablespoon water and the lemon juice. Cook over medium heat, stirring occasionally, until bubbly. Reduce heat to low; cover and cook 6 to 8 minutes, stirring occasionally, until apples are tender.

2 In small bowl, mix flour, 1 tablespoon granulated sugar and the salt. Gradually stir into apple mixture, cooking and stirring until mixture thickens. Remove from heat; stir in butter and vanilla. Cool 15 minutes.

3 Meanwhile, heat oven to 375°F. On ungreased cookie sheet, unroll pie crust. Spoon cooled filling evenly onto half of crust to within ½ inch of edge.

4 In small bowl, beat egg and 1 tablespoon water; brush over edge of crust. Fold untopped half of crust over filling; firmly press edge to seal. Flute edge; cut small slits or shapes in several places in top crust. Brush top with remaining egg mixture. In another small bowl, mix 1 teaspoon granulated sugar and the cinnamon; sprinkle over crust.

5 Bake 25 to 35 minutes or until crust is golden brown. Cool on cooling rack at least 10 minutes before serving.

High Altitude (3500–6500 ft): In step 5, bake 23 to 28 minutes.

1 Serving: Calories 380; Total Fat 18g (Saturated Fat 7g; Trans Fat 0g); Cholesterol 70mg; Sodium 410mg; Total Carbohydrate 51g (Dietary Fiber 0g) **Exchanges:** ½ Starch, 3 Other Carbohydrate, 3½ Fat **Carbohydrate Choices:** 3½

 Pie Tip Tart apples such as Granny Smith or Haralson make flavorful apple foldovers. Braeburn or Gala apples provide good texture and a slightly sweeter flavor.

bananas foster tart

Brenda Elsea | Tuscon, AZ | Bake-Off® Contest 38, 1998

Prep Time: 30 Minutes ✳ Start to Finish: 1 Hour ✳ 10 servings

CRUST

1 Pillsbury refrigerated pie
   crust (from 15-oz box),
   softened as directed on box

FILLING

2 medium bananas, cut into
   ¼-inch slices

4½ teaspoons light rum*

2 teaspoons grated orange
   peel

⅔ cup chopped pecans

⅔ cup packed brown sugar

¼ cup whipping cream

¼ cup butter or margarine

½ teaspoon vanilla

SERVE WITH, IF DESIRED

Vanilla ice cream

1 Heat oven to 450°F. Bake pie crust as directed on box for One-Crust Baked Shell, using 9-inch tart pan with removable bottom or 9-inch glass pie plate. Cool on cooling rack 15 minutes.

2 Meanwhile, in small bowl, gently mix bananas and rum to coat. Sprinkle orange peel evenly in bottom of cooled baked crust. Arrange bananas in single layer over peel. Sprinkle with pecans.

3 In 2-quart heavy saucepan, mix brown sugar, whipping cream and butter. Cook and stir over medium-high heat 2 to 3 minutes or until mixture boils. Cook 2 to 4 minutes longer, stirring constantly, until mixture has thickened and is deep golden brown. Remove from heat; stir in vanilla. Spoon warm filling over bananas and pecans. Cool 30 minutes. To remove tart from sides of pan, place the pan on a wide, short can and pull down the side of the pan (see page 80). If necessary, use a thin-bladed knife to loosen crust from the side of the pan. Serve warm or cool with ice cream. Cover and refrigerate any remaining tart.

✳To substitute for the rum, mix ½ teaspoon rum extract with 4 teaspoons water.

High Altitude (3500–6500 ft): No change.

1 Serving: Calories 290; Total Fat 17g (Saturated Fat 7g; Trans Fat 0g); Cholesterol 20mg; Sodium 130mg; Total Carbohydrate 31g (Dietary Fiber 1g) **Exchanges:** ½ Starch, 1½ Other Carbohydrate, 3½ Fat **Carbohydrate Choices:** 2

ginger-lemon-blueberry pie

Prep Time: 35 Minutes ✳ Start to Finish: 3 Hours 20 Minutes ✳ 8 servings

CRUST

1 box (15 oz) Pillsbury
  refrigerated pie crusts,
  softened as directed on box

6 teaspoons sugar

1 teaspoon half-and-half

FILLING

5 cups fresh blueberries

½ cup sugar

2 tablespoons chopped
  crystallized ginger

2 tablespoons quick-cooking
  tapioca

1 teaspoon grated lemon peel

1 tablespoon fresh lemon juice

1 Place foil or cookie sheet on oven rack below middle rack to catch any spills if the filling should bubble over during baking. Heat oven to 400°F.

2 Unroll 1 pie crust on work surface. Sprinkle top of crust with 1½ teaspoons of the sugar. With rolling pin, roll lightly to coat with sugar. Place, sugared side up, in 9-inch glass pie plate, and continue as directed on box for Two-Crust Pie.

3 In large bowl, mix filling ingredients; spoon into crust-lined pie plate. Top with second crust; seal edge and flute. Cut slits in several places in top crust. Brush top of crust with half-and-half; sprinkle with remaining 4½ teaspoons sugar. Cover crust edge with foil to prevent excessive browning.

4 Place pie on middle oven rack. Bake 35 to 45 minutes or until crust is golden brown and filling is bubbly, removing foil during last 15 minutes of baking. Cool on cooling rack at least 2 hours before serving.

High Altitude (3500–6500 ft): Heat oven to 425°F. In step 4, bake 45 to 55 minutes.

1 Serving: Calories 400; Total Fat 18g (Saturated Fat 4.5g; Trans Fat 3g); Cholesterol 0mg; Sodium 300mg; Total Carbohydrate 57g (Dietary Fiber 3g) **Exchanges:** 1 Starch, 3 Other Carbohydrate, 3½ Fat **Carbohydrate Choices:** 4

cherry-blueberry pie

Prep Time: 30 Minutes ✳ Start to Finish: 3 Hours 25 Minutes ✳ 8 servings

CRUST

1 box (15 oz) Pillsbury refrigerated pie crusts, softened as directed on box

FILLING

½ cup sugar

2 tablespoons cornstarch

¼ teaspoon ground cinnamon

1 can (21 oz) cherry pie filling

1½ cups fresh or frozen blueberries (do not thaw)

CRUST GLAZE

1 egg white

1 teaspoon water

2 teaspoons sugar

1 Heat oven to 425°F. Make pie crusts as directed on box for Two-Crust Pie, using 9-inch glass pie plate.

2 In large bowl, mix ½ cup sugar, the cornstarch and cinnamon. Stir in pie filling and blueberries; spoon into crust-lined pie plate. Top with second crust; seal edge and flute. Cut slits or shapes in several places in top crust.

3 In small bowl, beat egg white and water with fork until blended; brush over top of pie (discard any remaining egg white mixture). Sprinkle with 2 teaspoons sugar. Cover edge with foil to prevent excessive browning.

4 Bake 45 to 55 minutes or until crust is golden brown, removing foil during last 15 minutes of bake time. Cool on cooling rack at least 2 hours before serving.

High Altitude (3500–6500 ft): No change.

1 Serving: Calories 340; Total Fat 14g (Saturated Fat 5g; Trans Fat 0g); Cholesterol 5mg; Sodium 230mg; Total Carbohydrate 53g (Dietary Fiber 1g) **Exchanges:** ½ Starch, 3 Other Carbohydrate, 2½ Fat **Carbohydrate Choices:** 3½

Pie Tip For an extra-pretty pie, make decorative cutouts on the top crust. Use a small cookie or canapé cutter, and cut shapes from the top crust before placing it on the filling. Place the cutouts on top of the pie crust after brushing with egg glaze. Sprinkle with coarse sugar.

cherry–chocolate chip pie

Prep Time: 15 Minutes ✳ Start to Finish: 3 Hours 55 Minutes ✳ 8 servings

CRUST

1 box (15 oz) Pillsbury refrigerated pie crusts, softened as directed on box

½ cup sliced almonds

FILLING

2 cans (21 oz each) cherry pie filling

½ cup semisweet chocolate chips

1 teaspoon water

2 teaspoons sugar

1 Heat oven to 425°F. Make pie crusts as directed on box for Two-Crust Pie, using 9-inch glass pie plate. Reserve 1 tablespoon almonds; sprinkle remaining almonds in bottom of crust-lined pie plate.

2 In medium bowl, mix pie filling and chocolate chips. Spoon over almonds in pan. Top with second crust; seal edge and flute. Cut slits or shapes in several places in top crust. Brush water over top; sprinkle with reserved 1 tablespoon almonds and the sugar.

3 Cover crust edge with foil to prevent excessive browning. Bake 30 to 40 minutes or until crust is golden brown. Cool on cooling rack at least 3 hours before serving.

High Altitude (3500–6500 ft): Use 9-inch glass deep-dish pie plate. In step 3, bake 35 to 45 minutes.

1 Serving: Calories 500; Total Fat 22g (Saturated Fat 7g; Trans Fat 0g); Cholesterol 5mg; Sodium 220mg; Total Carbohydrate 71g (Dietary Fiber 4g) **Exchanges:** 1½ Starch, 3 Other Carbohydrate, 4½ Fat **Carbohydrate Choices:** 5

raspberry–chocolate chip pie: Substitute 2 cans (21 oz each) raspberry pie filling for the cherry pie filling.

berry–chocolate chip pie: Substitute 1 can (21 oz) raspberry pie filling for 1 can of the cherry pie filling.

crumble cherry-marzipan pie

Prep Time: 15 Minutes ✳ Start to Finish: 55 Minutes ✳ 8 servings

CRUST

1 Pillsbury refrigerated pie crust (from 15-oz box), softened as directed on box

FILLING

2 cans (21 oz each) cherry pie filling

¼ teaspoon almond extract

TOPPING

4 oz marzipan (about ⅓ cup)

3 tablespoons butter or margarine, softened

½ cup old-fashioned oats

2 tablespoons all-purpose flour

1 Heat oven to 375°F. Make pie crust as directed on box for One-Crust Baked Shell, using 9-inch glass pie plate—except bake 8 to 10 minutes or just until set but not brown.

2 Meanwhile, in large bowl, mix filling ingredients. In small bowl, place marzipan and butter; with pastry blender or fork, mix until well blended. Stir in oats and flour until crumbly.

3 Remove partially baked crust from oven. Pour filling into crust. Crumble topping over filling.

4 Return to oven; bake 30 to 40 minutes longer or until topping is golden brown and filling is bubbly around edges. If necessary, after 15 minutes of baking, cover crust edge with foil to prevent excessive browning.

High Altitude (3500–6500 ft): Use 9-inch glass deep-dish pie plate. In step 1, bake crust 10 to 12 minutes. In step 4, bake 35 to 45 minutes.

1 Serving: Calories 420; Total Fat 15g (Saturated Fat 6g; Trans Fat 0g); Cholesterol 15mg; Sodium 140mg; Total Carbohydrate 66g (Dietary Fiber 3g) **Exchanges:** 1½ Starch, 3 Other Carbohydrate, 2½ Fat **Carbohydrate Choices:** 4½

Pie Tip Marzipan is made from sugar and ground almonds. It's similar to almond paste, but it has a lower percentage of almonds. The rich almond flavor complements the cherries in this pie. Marzipan is also used to make edible cake decorations, such as flowers or fruits. You can find it in the baking aisle of your supermarket.

almond macaroon-cherry pie

Rose Anne LeMon | Sierra Vista, AZ | Bake-Off® Contest 32, 1986

Prep Time: 20 Minutes ✳ Start to Finish: 3 Hours 10 Minutes ✳ 8 servings

CRUST
1 Pillsbury refrigerated pie
   crust (from 15-oz box),
   softened as directed on box

FILLING
1 can (21 oz) cherry pie filling

¼ to ½ teaspoon ground
   cinnamon

⅛ teaspoon salt, if desired

1 teaspoon lemon juice

TOPPING
1 cup coconut

½ cup sliced almonds

¼ cup sugar

⅛ teaspoon salt, if desired

¼ cup milk

1 tablespoon butter or
   margarine, melted

¼ teaspoon almond extract

1 egg, beaten

1 Heat oven to 400°F. Place pie crust in 9-inch glass pie plate as directed on box for One-Crust Filled Pie.

2 In large bowl, mix filling ingredients; spoon into crust-lined pie plate. Cover edge with foil to prevent excessive browning. Bake 20 minutes.

3 Meanwhile, in medium bowl, mix topping ingredients. Spread topping evenly over pie.

4 Bake 15 to 30 minutes longer or until crust and topping are golden brown, removing foil during last 10 to 15 minutes of bake time. Cool on cooling rack at least 2 hours before serving.

High Altitude (3500–6500 ft): No change.

1 Serving: Calories 330; Total Fat 16g (Saturated Fat 7g; Trans Fat 0g); Cholesterol 35mg; Sodium 160mg; Total Carbohydrate 45g (Dietary Fiber 2g) **Exchanges:** 1 Starch, 2 Other Carbohydrate, 3 Fat **Carbohydrate Choices:** 3

raspberry-cherry pie

Prep Time: 35 Minutes ✳ Start to Finish: 3 Hours 20 Minutes ✳ 8 servings

CRUST

1 box (15 oz) Pillsbury refrigerated pie crusts, softened as directed on box

FILLING

2 cups fresh or frozen whole raspberries (do not thaw)

¼ to ½ cup sugar

1 tablespoon all-purpose flour

1 can (21 oz) cherry pie filling

1 Place foil or cookie sheet on oven rack below middle rack to catch any spills if the filling should bubble over during baking. Heat oven to 400°F. Make pie crusts as directed on box for Two-Crust Pie, using 9-inch glass pie plate.

2 In large bowl, gently mix filling ingredients; spoon into crust-lined pie plate. Top with second crust; seal edge and flute. Cut slits or shapes in several places in top crust. Cover edge with strips of foil to prevent excessive browning.

3 Bake 40 to 45 minutes or until crust is golden brown and filling is bubbly, removing foil during last 15 minutes of baking. Cool on cooling rack at least 2 hours before serving.

High Altitude (3500–6500 ft): Heat oven to 425°F. In step 3, bake 45 to 55 minutes.

1 Serving: Calories 390; Total Fat 18g (Saturated Fat 4.5g; Trans Fat 3g); Cholesterol 0mg; Sodium 300mg; Total Carbohydrate 53g (Dietary Fiber 4g) **Exchanges:** 1½ Starch, 2 Other Carbohydrate, 3½ Fat **Carbohydrate Choices:** 3½

blueberry-cherry pie: Substitute 2 cups fresh or frozen blueberries (do not thaw) for the raspberries.

raspberry-lemon cream pie with almond crust

Prep Time: 25 Minutes ✳ Start to Finish: 3 Hours 50 Minutes ✳ 8 servings

CRUST
1 package (7 oz) almond paste

1 tablespoon cornstarch

1 egg white

1 box (15 oz) Pillsbury refrigerated pie crusts, softened as directed on box

FILLING
1 can (14 oz) sweetened condensed milk (not evaporated)

2 tablespoons grated lemon peel (2 medium)

⅓ cup lemon juice (2 medium)

3 egg yolks

TOPPING
½ cup raspberry jelly or jam

¾ cup whipping cream

1 tablespoon powdered sugar

¼ teaspoon vanilla

¼ cup sliced almonds

Fresh raspberries, if desired

1 Heat oven to 400°F. Into food processor or medium bowl, crumble almond paste; add cornstarch and egg white. Cover; process with food processor, or beat with electric mixer, until smooth.

2 In 9-inch glass pie plate, unroll 1 pie crust. Press crust firmly against side and bottom of pie plate. Spread almond mixture evenly over crust. Unroll second pie crust over filling by starting at 1 edge of pie and unrolling to opposite edge. Press pie crusts together in bottom of pie plate. Seal edges and flute. Cover outer edge with foil; fit second pie plate inside first pie plate on top of crust. Bake 10 minutes. Remove top pie plate; gently prick crust surface over filling about 15 times with fork. Leave foil on outer edge. Bake uncovered about 15 minutes longer or until top crust begins to brown.

3 Meanwhile, in medium bowl, mix condensed milk, lemon peel, lemon juice and egg yolks with whisk. Pour over hot crust. Reduce oven temperature to 350°F. Bake 25 to 30 minutes longer or until filling is set and bottom crust is golden brown. Remove foil; cool completely on cooling rack, about 2 hours 30 minutes.

4 Spread jam over filling. In chilled deep small bowl, beat whipping cream, powdered sugar and vanilla with electric mixer on high speed until stiff peaks form. Spread over jam. Sprinkle with almonds and raspberries. Cover and refrigerate any remaining pie.

High Altitude (3500–6500 ft): No change.

1 Serving: Calories 680; Total Fat 35g (Saturated Fat 13g; Trans Fat 0g); Cholesterol 125mg; Sodium 310mg; Total Carbohydrate 84g (Dietary Fiber 2g) **Exchanges:** ½ Starch, 5 Other Carbohydrate, 1 High-Fat Meat, 5½ Fat **Carbohydrate Choices:** 5½

Pie Tip If you don't own two glass pie plates, purchase a disposable foil pie pan to place on top of the crust.

orchard medley pie

Prep Time: 20 Minutes ✳ Start to Finish: 3 Hours 10 Minutes ✳ 8 servings

FILLING

1½ cups diced peeled apples

¾ cup fresh red raspberries

¾ cup fresh blackberries

¾ cup fresh blueberries

¾ cup chopped rhubarb

¾ cup sugar

3 tablespoons quick-cooking tapioca

1 tablespoon lemon juice

1½ tablespoons cold butter or margarine, cut into small pieces

CRUST

1 box (15 oz) Pillsbury refrigerated pie crusts, softened as directed on box

1 Place foil or cookie sheet on oven rack below middle rack to catch any spills if the filling should bubble over during baking. Heat oven to 400°F. In large bowl, stir together filling ingredients. Let stand 15 minutes, stirring occasionally.

2 Make pie crusts as directed on box for Two-Crust Pie, using 9-inch glass pie plate. Spoon filling into crust-lined pie plate; dot with butter. Top with second crust; seal edge and flute. Cut slits or shapes in several places in top crust. Cover crust edge with foil to prevent excessive browning.

3 Bake 15 minutes; reduce oven temperature to 350°F. Bake 30 to 35 minutes longer or until filling bubbles in slits, removing foil during last 15 minutes of bake time. Cool on cooling rack at least 2 hours before serving.

High Altitude (3500–6500 ft): No change.

1 Serving: Calories 370; Total Fat 16g (Saturated Fat 6g; Trans Fat 0g); Cholesterol 15mg; Sodium 240mg; Total Carbohydrate 56g (Dietary Fiber 2g) **Exchanges:** ½ Fruit, 3½ Other Carbohydrate, 3 Fat **Carbohydrate Choices:** 4

 For a decorative top on your pie (see cover photo), cut off overhang of crust in pie plate to be even with plate edge. Spoon filling into crust-lined pie plate; dot with butter. Cut second crust into 1- to 1½-inch squares using fluted pastry wheel. Place squares over top of pie, pressing edge pieces gently into bottom crust edge. If desired, brush squares with milk and sprinkle with coarse or granulated sugar. Bake the pie as directed.

fresh strawberry pie

Prep Time: 30 Minutes ✳ Start to Finish: 4 Hours ✳ 8 servings

CRUST
1 Pillsbury refrigerated pie crust (from 15-oz box), softened as directed on box

FILLING
3 pints (6 cups) fresh strawberries

1 cup sugar

3 tablespoons cornstarch

½ cup water

4 to 5 drops red food color, if desired

TOPPING
1 cup sweetened whipped cream

1 Heat oven to 450°F. Bake pie crust as directed on box for One-Crust Baked Shell, using 9-inch glass pie plate. Cool completely on cooling rack, about 15 minutes.

2 Meanwhile, in small bowl, crush enough strawberries to make 1 cup. In 2-quart saucepan, mix sugar and cornstarch; stir in crushed strawberries and water. Cook, stirring constantly, until mixture boils and thickens. Stir in food color. Cool completely, about 30 minutes.

3 Place remaining strawberries, whole or sliced, in cooled baked crust. Pour cooked strawberry mixture evenly over berries. Refrigerate until set, about 3 hours, before serving.

4 Just before serving, top pie with sweetened whipped cream. Cover and refrigerate any remaining pie.

High Altitude (3500–6500 ft): No change.

1 Serving: Calories 340; Total Fat 14g (Saturated Fat 5g; Trans Fat 1.5g); Cholesterol 15mg; Sodium 150mg; Total Carbohydrate 51g (Dietary Fiber 3g) **Exchanges:** 1 Starch, 2½ Other Carbohydrate, 2½ Fat **Carbohydrate Choices:** 3½

fresh peach pie: Substitute 6 cups sliced peeled fresh peaches for the strawberries. Omit red food color.

fresh raspberry pie: Substitute 6 cups fresh raspberries for the strawberries.

strawberry-cherry pie

Prep Time: 30 Minutes ✳ Start to Finish: 2 Hours 30 Minutes ✳ 8 servings

CRUST
1 Pillsbury refrigerated pie crust (from 15-oz box), softened as directed on box

FILLING
1 package (8 oz) cream cheese, softened

⅓ cup sugar

1 teaspoon vanilla

½ teaspoon grated lemon peel

1 pint (2 cups) fresh whole strawberries

1 can (21 oz) cherry pie filling

SERVE WITH, IF DESIRED
Sweetened whipped cream

1 Heat oven to 450°F. Bake pie crust as directed on box for One-Crust Baked Shell, using 9-inch glass pie plate. Cool completely on cooling rack, about 15 minutes.

2 In small bowl, beat cream cheese, sugar, vanilla and lemon peel with electric mixer on medium speed until smooth and well blended. Spread evenly in cooled baked crust.

3 Arrange strawberries over cream cheese mixture; press in lightly. Spoon pie filling over strawberries. Refrigerate at least 2 hours before serving. Serve with whipped cream. Cover and refrigerate any remaining pie.

High Altitude (3500–6500 ft): No change.

1 Serving: Calories 340; Total Fat 18g (Saturated Fat 9g; Trans Fat 0g); Cholesterol 35mg; Sodium 190mg; Total Carbohydrate 43g (Dietary Fiber 2g) **Exchanges:** 1 Starch, ½ Fruit, 1½ Other Carbohydrate, 3½ Fat **Carbohydrate Choices:** 3

Pie Tip This is a good pie for entertaining because it's colorful and can be made the night before. Loosely cover with plastic wrap, and refrigerate it until serving time.

stuffed-crust strawberry cream pie

Prep Time: 25 Minutes ✷ Start to Finish: 2 Hours 35 Minutes ✷ 8 servings

CRUST

1 box (15 oz) Pillsbury refrigerated pie crusts, softened as directed on box

1 package (7 oz) almond paste

1 teaspoon cornstarch

1 egg white

FILLING

½ cup granulated sugar

3 tablespoons cornstarch

3 cups sliced fresh strawberries*

TOPPING

1 cup whipping cream

2 tablespoons powdered sugar

¼ teaspoon vanilla

8 fresh whole strawberries, if desired

1 Heat oven to 400°F. Unroll 1 pie crust on work surface. Into medium bowl or food processor, crumble almond paste. Add 1 teaspoon cornstarch and the egg white. Mix or cover and process until smooth. Spread evenly on crust to within 1¼ inches of edge. Unroll second crust; place on top and pat together gently. Place stuffed crust in ungreased 9-inch glass pie plate. Seal edges and flute. Cover crust edge with foil; fit second pie plate inside first pie plate on top of crust.

2 Bake 10 minutes. Remove top pie plate; gently prick crust surface over filling about 15 times with fork. Bake uncovered about 15 minutes longer or until crust is light golden brown. Cool completely on cooling rack, about 1 hour.

3 Meanwhile, in 2-quart saucepan, mix granulated sugar and 3 tablespoons cornstarch. Stir in strawberries. Heat to boiling over medium heat, stirring constantly. Cook and stir 3 to 5 minutes or until filling thickens. Refrigerate about 30 minutes, stirring once, until cool.

4 Just before serving, spread strawberry filling evenly in crust. In medium bowl, beat whipping cream, powdered sugar and vanilla with electric mixer on high speed until soft peaks form. Spread on top of pie. Garnish with strawberries.

✱One bag (1 lb) frozen unsweetened strawberries, sliced and thawed, can be used instead of the fresh.

High Altitude (3500–6500 ft): No change.

1 Serving: Calories 540; Total Fat 30g (Saturated Fat 11g; Trans Fat 0g); Cholesterol 40mg; Sodium 240mg; Total Carbohydrate 63g (Dietary Fiber 3g) **Exchanges:** 1 Starch, 3 Other Carbohydrate, 6 Fat **Carbohydrate Choices:** 4

Pie Tip If you don't own two pie plates, purchase a disposable foil pie pan to place on top of the crust.

rustic strawberry tart with strawberry cream

Prep Time: 35 Minutes ✳ Start to Finish: 35 Minutes ✳ 8 servings

CRUST

1 Pillsbury refrigerated pie crust (from 15-oz box), softened as directed on box

FILLING

2 tablespoons granulated sugar

1 tablespoon cornstarch

3¼ cups coarsely chopped fresh strawberries*

1 teaspoon granulated sugar

TOPPING

½ cup whipping cream

1 tablespoon powdered sugar

1 Heat oven to 450°F. Lightly spray cookie sheet with cooking spray. Unroll pie crust on cookie sheet.

2 In medium bowl, mix 2 tablespoons granulated sugar and the cornstarch. Gently stir in 3 cups of the strawberries. Spoon onto center of crust, spreading evenly to within 2 inches of edge. Carefully fold 2-inch crust edge up over filling, pleating crust slightly as necessary. Brush crust edge with water; sprinkle with 1 teaspoon granulated sugar.

3 Bake 15 to 20 minutes or until crust is golden brown.

4 Meanwhile, in small bowl, beat whipping cream and powdered sugar with electric mixer on high speed until stiff peaks form. In another small bowl, mash remaining ¼ cup strawberries; fold into whipped cream. Serve topping with tart.

*Frozen strawberries are not recommended for this recipe because they would add too much moisture to the tart.

High Altitude (3500–6500 ft): No change.

1 Serving: Calories 210; Total Fat 12g (Saturated Fat 5g; Trans Fat 0g); Cholesterol 20mg; Sodium 115mg; Total Carbohydrate 24g (Dietary Fiber 2g) **Exchanges:** 1½ Other Carbohydrate, 2½ Fat **Carbohydrate Choices:** 1½

fresh strawberry tarts

Prep Time: 45 Minutes ✳ Start to Finish: 1 Hour 15 Minutes ✳ 6 tarts

CRUST

1 Pillsbury refrigerated pie
crust (from 15-oz box),
softened as directed on box

¾ teaspoon sugar

FILLING

2½ cups sliced fresh
strawberries

½ cup strawberry pie glaze

6 tablespoons hot fudge
topping, heated

⅓ cup frozen (thawed)
whipped topping

1 Heat oven to 450°F. Spray back of 12-cup regular-size muffin pan with cooking spray. Unroll pie crust on work surface. Sprinkle crust with sugar; press in lightly.

2 Cut 6 rounds from crust with 4-inch round cookie cutter, or trace 6 rounds with top of large drinking glass and cut out with sharp knife (if necessary, piece pie crust scraps together for sixth round).

3 Fit rounds, sugared side up, alternately over backs of muffin cups. Pinch 5 equally spaced pleats around side of each cup. Prick each generously with fork.

4 Bake 5 to 7 minutes or until lightly browned. Cool 5 minutes. Carefully remove tart shells from muffin cups. Cool completely, about 30 minutes.

5 Meanwhile, in large bowl, gently mix strawberries and pie glaze. Refrigerate until thoroughly chilled, about 30 minutes.

6 Just before serving, spoon 1 tablespoon warm fudge topping into each tart shell. Spoon about ⅓ cup berry mixture over topping in each; top with whipped topping.

High Altitude (3500–6500 ft): In step 4, bake 5 to 6 minutes.

1 Tart: Calories 330; Total Fat 12g (Saturated Fat 4.5g; Trans Fat 0g); Cholesterol 5mg; Sodium 220mg; Total Carbohydrate 54g (Dietary Fiber 3g) **Exchanges:** 3½ Other Carbohydrate, 2½ Fat **Carbohydrate Choices:** 3½

Pie Tip It's best to use strawberries soon after you purchase them. To store for a day or two, arrange unwashed berries in a single layer in a pan lined with paper towels. Cover the berries with paper towels and refrigerate; wash just before use.

individual mixed-berry pies

Prep Time: 10 Minutes ✳ Start to Finish: 1 Hour 5 Minutes ✳ 4 pies

FILLING

1 cup frozen unsweetened whole strawberries, thawed

¾ cup frozen unsweetened blueberries, thawed

¾ cup frozen unsweetened raspberries, thawed

⅓ cup sugar

2 tablespoons cornstarch

CRUST

1 Pillsbury refrigerated pie crust (from 15-oz box), softened as directed on box

1 teaspoon sugar

1 Heat oven to 425°F. In large bowl, mix filling ingredients. Divide filling mixture evenly among 4 (6-oz) custard cups or ramekins.

2 Unroll pie crust on work surface. Cut 4 (5-inch) rounds from pie crust. Place each round over pie filling, draping over edges of custard cups. Cut slits or shapes on top of each. Sprinkle with 1 teaspoon sugar. Place custard cups on cookie sheet.

3 Bake 17 to 23 minutes or until edges are deep golden brown and centers are thoroughly baked. Cool on cooling rack about 30 minutes. Serve warm.

High Altitude (3500–6500 ft): No change.

1 Pie: Calories 330; Total Fat 11g (Saturated Fat 4g; Trans Fat 0g); Cholesterol 5mg; Sodium 170mg; Total Carbohydrate 57g (Dietary Fiber 5g) **Exchanges:** ½ Fruit, 3½ Other Carbohydrate, 2 Fat **Carbohydrate Choices:** 4

Pie Tip These are great little pies to make during the months when fresh berries aren't at their peak. But during berry season you may want to make them using fresh berries instead of frozen.

streusel-topped peach pie

Prep Time: 35 Minutes ✳ Start to Finish: 1 Hour 20 Minutes ✳ 8 servings

CRUST

1 Pillsbury refrigerated pie crust (from 15-oz box), softened as directed on box

FILLING

½ cup powdered sugar

⅓ cup all-purpose flour

½ teaspoon ground cinnamon

4 cups sliced peeled peaches (6 medium)*

STREUSEL

¾ cup all-purpose flour

½ cup packed brown sugar

½ teaspoon ground cinnamon

⅓ cup cold butter or margarine

1 Heat oven to 375°F. Place pie crust in 9-inch glass pie plate as directed on box for One-Crust Filled Pie.

2 In large bowl, mix powdered sugar, ⅓ cup flour and ½ teaspoon cinnamon. Gently stir in peaches until coated. Spoon into crust-lined pie plate.

3 In medium bowl, mix ¾ cup flour, the brown sugar and ½ teaspoon cinnamon. Cut in butter, using pastry blender (or fork or pulling 2 table knives through mixture in opposite directions), until mixture looks like coarse crumbs. Sprinkle strusel evenly over filling.

4 Bake 40 to 45 minutes or until strusel is golden brown. Cover crust edge with foil after 15 or 20 minutes of baking to prevent excessive browning.

*Two cans (29 oz each) peach slices, well drained, can be substituted for the fresh sliced peaches.

High Altitude (3500–6500 ft): In step 4, bake 53 to 58 minutes.

1 Serving: Calories 360; Total Fat 15g (Saturated Fat 7g; Trans Fat 0g); Cholesterol 25mg; Sodium 170mg; Total Carbohydrate 54g (Dietary Fiber 2g) **Exchanges:** ½ Starch, ½ Fruit, 2½ Other Carbohydrate, 3 Fat **Carbohydrate Choices:** 3½

streusel-topped peach-blueberry pie: Substitute 1 cup fresh or frozen blueberries (do not thaw) for 1 cup of the peaches.

southern peach-almond pie with berry sauce

Prep Time: 30 Minutes ✳ Start to Finish: 3 Hours ✳ 8 servings

CRUST

1 box (15 oz) Pillsbury refrigerated pie crusts, softened as directed on box

1 tablespoon sliced almonds, if desired

FILLING

5½ to 6 cups sliced peeled peaches (8 to 9 medium)

1 tablespoon lemon juice

1 cup sugar

¼ cup cornstarch

¼ teaspoon ground nutmeg

¼ teaspoon salt

SAUCE

¼ cup sugar

1 tablespoon cornstarch

1 bag (12 oz) frozen whole raspberries or blackberries, thawed, drained and liquid reserved

½ teaspoon almond extract

1 Heat oven to 400°F. Make pie crusts as directed on box for Two-Crust Pie, using 9-inch glass pie plate. Sprinkle sliced almonds over second crust; roll in with rolling pin.

2 In large bowl, gently mix peaches and lemon juice to coat. Gently stir in remaining filling ingredients. Spoon into crust-lined pie plate. Carefully place second crust, almond side up, over filling; seal edge and flute. Cut slits or shapes in several places in top crust.

3 Bake 35 to 45 minutes or until golden brown. Cover crust edge with foil after 15 to 20 minutes of bake time to prevent excessive browning. Cool on cooling rack at least 1 hour before serving.

4 Meanwhile, in 2-quart saucepan, mix ¼ cup sugar and 1 tablespoon cornstarch. If necessary, add water to reserved raspberry liquid to measure ½ cup. Gradually stir liquid into sugar mixture, cooking and stirring over medium heat until thickened. Gently fold in raspberries; stir in almond extract. Cool completely, about 1 hour. Serve sauce with pie.

High Altitude (3500–6500 ft): In step 3, bake 45 to 55 minutes.

1 Serving: Calories 470; Total Fat 14g (Saturated Fat 5g; Trans Fat 0g); Cholesterol 5mg; Sodium 300mg; Total Carbohydrate 84g (Dietary Fiber 3g) **Exchanges:** ½ Fruit, 5 Other Carbohydrate, 3 Fat **Carbohydrate Choices:** 5½

Pie Tip For easier peeling, submerge peaches in boiling water for about 30 seconds; remove them with a slotted spoon and transfer to ice water—the skins will slide off more easily.

amaretto peach tart

Prep Time: 35 Minutes ✳ Start to Finish: 2 Hours 40 Minutes ✳ 10 servings

CRUST

1 Pillsbury refrigerated pie
   crust (from 15-oz box),
   softened as directed on box

FILLING

1 package (8 oz) cream cheese,
   softened

⅓ cup sugar

2 tablespoons amaretto or
   ¼ teaspoon almond extract

2 eggs

TOPPING

2 tablespoons peach preserves

1 tablespoon amaretto or
   ⅛ teaspoon almond extract

2 cups thinly sliced peeled
   peaches (3 medium)*

1 Heat oven to 450°F. Bake pie crust as directed on box for One-Crust Baked Shell, using 10-inch tart pan with removable bottom. Cool completely on cooling rack, about 15 minutes.

2 Reduce oven temperature to 375°F. In medium bowl, beat cream cheese and sugar with electric mixer on medium speed until light and fluffy. Beat in 2 tablespoons amaretto and the eggs until well blended. Pour into cooled baked crust.

3 Bake at 375°F 18 to 22 minutes or until filling is set. Cool on cooling rack 10 minutes. Refrigerate at least 1 hour until completely cooled and set.

4 Just before serving, in medium microwave bowl, microwave preserves on High 20 seconds. Stir in 1 tablespoon amaretto. Stir in peaches to coat. Arrange peach slices over top of tart. To remove tart from sides of pan, place the pan on a wide, short can and pull down the side of the pan (see page 80). If necessary, use a thin-bladed knife to loosen crust from the side of the pan. Cover and refrigerate any remaining tart.

*One package (16 oz) frozen sliced peaches without syrup, thawed and well drained, can be substituted for the 2 cups fresh sliced peaches.

High Altitude (3500–6500 ft): No change.

1 Serving: Calories 250; Total Fat 15g (Saturated Fat 7g; Trans Fat 0g); Cholesterol 70mg; Sodium 170mg; Total Carbohydrate 25g (Dietary Fiber 0g) **Exchanges:** 1 Starch, ½ Other Carbohydrate, 3 Fat **Carbohydrate Choices:** 1½

plum peachy pie

Prep Time: 25 Minutes ✳ Start to Finish: 2 Hours 45 Minutes ✳ 8 servings

CRUST

1 box (15 oz) Pillsbury refrigerated pie crusts, softened as directed on box

FILLING

1 tablespoon peach-flavored gelatin (from a box)

¼ cup cornstarch

1 cup sugar

4 cups sliced peeled fresh peaches (6 medium) or frozen (thawed) sliced peaches

2 medium red plums, pitted, peeled and thinly sliced

1 tablespoon cold butter or margarine, cut into small pieces

½ teaspoon sugar

1 Heat oven to 400°F. Make pie crusts as directed on box for Two-Crust Pie, using 9-inch glass pie plate.

2 In large bowl, mix gelatin, cornstarch and 1 cup sugar; gently stir in peaches until evenly coated. Spoon into crust-lined pie plate. Top with plum slices. Dot with butter. Top with second crust; seal edge and flute. Cut slits or shapes in several places in top crust.

3 Brush small amount of water over top crust; sprinkle lightly with ½ teaspoon sugar. Cover crust edge with foil to prevent excessive browning.

4 Bake 10 minutes. Reduce oven to 350°F; bake 35 to 40 minutes longer or until crust is golden brown and peaches are tender. Cool on cooling rack 1 hour 30 minutes before serving.

High Altitude (3500–6500 ft): In step 4, increase second bake time to 40 to 45 minutes.

1 Serving: Calories 410; Total Fat 16g (Saturated Fat 6g; Trans Fat 0g); Cholesterol 10mg; Sodium 240mg; Total Carbohydrate 66g (Dietary Fiber 1g) **Exchanges:** ½ Fruit, 4 Other Carbohydrate, 3 Fat **Carbohydrate Choices:** 4½

Pie Tip The addition of the 1 tablespoon peach-flavored gelatin thickens the filling upon cooling and also bumps up the peach flavor.

peach dumplings with raspberry sauce

Prep Time: 15 Minutes ✳ Start to Finish: 50 Minutes ✳ 4 servings

DUMPLINGS

1 Pillsbury refrigerated pie crust (from 15-oz box), softened as directed on box

1 can (16 oz) peach halves in light syrup, drained, liquid reserved

1 egg white, slightly beaten

1 tablespoon sugar

SAUCE

½ cup red raspberry preserves

¼ teaspoon almond extract

1 Heat oven to 425°F. Unroll pie crust on work surface. Cut crust into quarters.

2 Divide peaches evenly onto crust quarters. Brush crust edges lightly with reserved peach liquid. Bring sides of each crust quarter up over peaches; press edges to seal, making 3 seams. Place seam side up in ungreased 8-inch square or 12×8-inch (2-quart) glass baking dish. Brush with egg white; sprinkle with sugar.

3 Bake 22 to 32 minutes or until golden brown. Immediately remove from baking dish; place in individual dessert dishes.

4 In 1-quart saucepan, mix preserves and almond extract. Heat over low heat, stirring occasionally, until warm. Serve warm dumplings with sauce.

High Altitude (3500–6500 ft): In step 3, bake 22 to 27 minutes.

1 Serving: Calories 400; Total Fat 14g (Saturated Fat 5g; Trans Fat 0g); Cholesterol 5mg; Sodium 250mg; Total Carbohydrate 67g (Dietary Fiber 1g) **Exchanges:** ½ Starch, 4 Other Carbohydrate, 2½ Fat **Carbohydrate Choices:** 4½

fresh pear crostata

Prep Time: 25 Minutes ✳ Start to Finish: 1 Hour ✳ 8 servings

CRUST

1 Pillsbury refrigerated pie crust (from 15-oz box), softened as directed on box

FILLING

½ cup sugar

3 tablespoons all-purpose flour

4 cups chopped peeled ripe pears (8 to 9 medium)

TOPPING

1 teaspoon sugar

2 tablespoons sliced almonds

1 Heat oven to 450°F. In ungreased 15×10×1-inch pan, unroll pie crust.

2 In medium bowl, mix ½ cup sugar and the flour. Gently stir in pears to coat. Spoon pear mixture onto center of crust to within 2 inches of edge. Carefully fold 2-inch edge of crust up over pear mixture, pleating crust slightly as necessary. Sprinkle 1 teaspoon sugar over crust edge.

3 Bake 14 to 20 minutes, sprinkling almonds over pear mixture during last 5 minutes of bake time, until pears are tender and crust is golden brown. Cool on cooling rack 15 minutes. Cut into wedges; serve warm. Cover and refrigerate any remaining crostata.

High Altitude (3500–6500 ft): In step 3, bake 20 to 26 minutes.

1 Serving: Calories 240; Total Fat 8g (Saturated Fat 2.5g; Trans Fat 0g); Cholesterol 0mg; Sodium 110mg; Total Carbohydrate 41g (Dietary Fiber 3g) **Exchanges:** ½ Fruit, 2 Other Carbohydrate, 2 Fat **Carbohydrate Choices:** 3

fresh apple crostata: Substitute 4 cups chopped peeled cooking apples (4 medium) for the pears.

Pie Tip Hungry for a pear crostata but all the pears are rock hard? To speed up the ripening process, place them in a paper bag with an apple. Pierce the bag in several places with the tip of a knife, and leave at room temperature.

pear-walnut crumble pie

Prep Time: 20 Minutes ✳ Start to Finish: 1 Hour 35 Minutes ✳ 8 servings

CRUST

1 Pillsbury refrigerated pie
  crust (from 15-oz box),
  softened as directed on box

FILLING

5 cups sliced peeled pears
  (5 large)

2 tablespoons granulated
  sugar

1 tablespoon all-purpose flour

1 teaspoon grated lemon peel

¼ teaspoon ground ginger

Dash salt

TOPPING

½ cup all-purpose flour

⅓ cup packed brown sugar

½ teaspoon ground cinnamon

¼ teaspoon ground ginger

¼ teaspoon ground nutmeg

⅓ cup cold butter or
  margarine, cut into pieces

½ cup chopped walnuts

1 Heat oven to 400°F. Place pie crust in 9-inch glass pie plate as directed on box for One-Crust Filled Pie.

2 In large bowl, lightly toss filling ingredients. If pears are very juicy, add additional 1 tablespoon flour. Spoon into crust-lined pie plate.

3 In medium bowl, mix ½ cup flour, the brown sugar, cinnamon, ¼ teaspoon ginger and nutmeg. Cut in butter, using pastry blender (or fork or pulling two knives through mixture in oppposite directions), until mixture is crumbly. Stir in walnuts. Spoon over filling.

4 Cover crust edge with foil to prevent excessive browning. Bake 35 to 45 minutes or until topping is golden brown. Cool at least 30 minutes before serving. Serve warm or cool.

High Altitude (3500–6500 ft): In step 4, bake 40 to 50 minutes.

1 Serving: Calories 370; Total Fat 20g (Saturated Fat 8g; Trans Fat 0g); Cholesterol 25mg; Sodium 190mg; Total Carbohydrate 47g (Dietary Fiber 3g) **Exchanges:** ½ Starch, 1 Fruit, 1½ Other Carbohydrate, 4 Fat **Carbohydrate Choices:** 3

Pie Tip The juiciness of pears varies quite a bit according to variety and ripeness. If the pears are dripping juice when you slice them, cut them slightly thick and use 2 tablespoons of flour. If they are firm and dry, slice them thinly and use only 1 tablespoon of flour.

ginger-pear pie

Prep Time: 20 Minutes ✳ Start to Finish: 1 Hour 40 Minutes ✳ 8 servings

CRUST

1 box (15 oz) Pillsbury refrigerated pie crusts, softened as directed on box

¼ cup apricot preserves

⅓ cup crushed gingersnap cookies (about 7 cookies)

FILLING

6 cups thinly sliced, peeled pears (6 large)

2 teaspoons grated gingerroot

¼ cup packed brown sugar

2 tablespoons cold butter or margarine, cut into small pieces

GLAZE

½ cup powdered sugar

2 teaspoons milk

¼ teaspoon vanilla

1 Heat oven to 400°F. Make pie crusts as directed on box for Two-Crust Pie, using 9-inch glass pie plate. Spread preserves over bottom of crust in pie plate; sprinkle with cookie crumbs.

2 In large bowl, mix pears, gingerroot and brown sugar. Spoon filling evenly over crumbs. Dot with butter. Top with second crust; seal edge and flute. Cut slits or shapes in several places in top crust.

3 Cover crust edge with foil to prevent excessive browning. Bake 15 minutes. Reduce oven temperature to 350°F. Bake 40 to 45 minutes longer or until bubbly and top is golden brown. Remove foil; cool on cooling rack about 20 minutes.

4 Meanwhile, in small bowl, mix glaze ingredients. Gently brush glaze over top of warm pie. Serve warm or cool.

High Altitude (3500–6500 ft): Increase second bake time in step 3 to 50 to 55 minutes.

1 Serving: Calories 430; Total Fat 18g (Saturated Fat 7g; Trans Fat 0g); Cholesterol 15mg; Sodium 280mg; Total Carbohydrate 68g (Dietary Fiber 3g) **Exchanges:** ½ Starch, 1 Fruit, 3 Other Carbohydrate, 3½ Fat **Carbohydrate Choices:** 4½

 Pie Tip For a holiday pie, omit the glaze. Instead, brush the unbaked pie with 2 tablespoons of milk; sprinkle with orange decorator sugar crystals for Halloween or Thanksgiving, or red or green for Christmas.

rhu-berry pie

Prep Time: 25 Minutes ✳ Start to Finish: 2 Hours 10 Minutes ✳ 8 servings

CRUST
1 box (15 oz) Pillsbury
   refrigerated pie crusts,
   softened as directed on box

FILLING
2 cups cut-up fresh rhubarb*

2 cups fresh blueberries*

¾ cup sugar

¼ cup all-purpose flour

⅛ teaspoon ground nutmeg

Dash salt

2 teaspoons milk

1 tablespoon coarse sugar, if
   desired

1 Heat oven to 400°F. Make pie crusts as directed on box for Two-Crust Pie, using 9-inch glass pie plate.

2 In large bowl, mix filling ingredients except milk and coarse sugar; toss gently to mix. Spoon into crust-lined pie plate.

3 Unroll second crust on work surface. Cut crust into about 2×1½-inch rectangles. Place in straight rows across filling, placing one corner over the other, leaving about 1 inch between rows. Place remaining dough rectangles around edge, overlapping to fit. Brush with milk; sprinkle with coarse sugar. Cover crust edge with foil to prevent excessive browning.

4 Bake 42 to 46 minutes or until filling bubbles in middle and crust is golden brown, removing foil during last 15 to 20 minutes of bake time. Cool on cooling rack at least 1 hour before serving.

*Two cups cut-up frozen rhubarb and 2 cups frozen blueberries can be substituted for the fresh rhubarb and blueberries.

High Altitude (3500–6500 ft): In step 4, bake 46 to 50 minutes.

1 Serving: Calories 350; Total Fat 14g (Saturated Fat 5g; Trans Fat 0g); Cholesterol 10mg; Sodium 240mg; Total Carbohydrate 54g (Dietary Fiber 1g) **Exchanges:** 3½ Other Carbohydrate, 3 Fat **Carbohydrate Choices:** 3½

 Get creative with the crust! Instead of rectangles, cut the second crust into shapes using a small cookie cutter to cut hearts, circles or other shapes. Place the shapes across the filling leaving space between each shape. Place any remaining shapes around the edge, overlapping to fit if necessary.

country rhubarb pie

Prep Time: 20 Minutes ✱ Start to Finish: 4 Hours 20 Minutes ✱ 8 servings

CRUST
1 Pillsbury refrigerated pie crust (from 15-oz box), softened as directed on box

FILLING
1 cup sugar

3 tablespoons all-purpose flour

½ teaspoon grated orange peel

3 eggs, slightly beaten

½ cup sour cream

3½ cups sliced fresh rhubarb*

TOPPING
¼ cup sugar

¼ cup all-purpose flour

2 tablespoons butter or margarine, softened

1 Heat oven to 375°F. Place pie crust in 9-inch glass pie plate as directed on box for One-Crust Filled Pie (do not trim or flute crust).

2 In medium bowl, mix 1 cup sugar, 3 tablespoons flour and the orange peel. Stir in eggs and sour cream. Add rhubarb; toss gently. Spoon into crust-lined pie plate. Fold edges of crust over filling, pleating crust slightly as necessary.

3 In small bowl, mix topping ingredients until crumbly. Sprinkle over filling.

4 Bake 50 to 60 minutes or until crust is light golden brown. Cool on cooling rack 3 hours before serving. Cover and refrigerate any remaining pie.

✱Three and a half cups sliced frozen rhubarb (do not thaw) can be substituted for the fresh rhubarb.

High Altitude (3500–6500 ft): In step 4, bake 55 to 65 minutes.

1 Serving: Calories 350; Total Fat 15g (Saturated Fat 7g; Trans Fat 0g); Cholesterol 100mg; Sodium 160mg; Total Carbohydrate 51g (Dietary Fiber 0g) **Exchanges:** ½ Starch, 3 Other Carbohydrate, 3 Fat **Carbohydrate Choices:** 3½

Pie Tip When choosing rhubarb, pick out crisp, brightly colored stalks. The deeper the red, the more flavorful the rhubarb stalks are likely to be. Medium-size stalks are generally more tender than large ones, which may be stringy. Rhubarb, when tightly wrapped in a plastic bag, should keep up to 3 days in the refrigerator. To prepare fresh rhubarb, trim the ends and discard all traces of the leaves (rhubarb leaves are poisonous). Wash the stalks and cut into pieces.

rhubarb crunch pie

Prep Time: 25 Minutes ✳ Start to Finish: 4 Hours 30 Minutes ✳ 8 servings

FILLING

5 cups sliced fresh rhubarb*

¾ cup sugar

3 tablespoons quick-cooking tapioca

1 to 2 teaspoons grated orange peel

CRUST

1 Pillsbury refrigerated pie crust (from 15-oz box), softened as directed on box

STREUSEL

½ cup all-purpose flour

½ cup sugar

6 tablespoons cold butter or margarine

1 Place foil or cookie sheet on oven rack below middle rack to catch any spills if the filling should bubble over during baking. Heat oven to 400°F. In large bowl, mix filling ingredients; let stand 15 minutes.

2 Place pie crust in 9-inch glass pie plate as directed on box for One-Crust Filled Pie.

3 In small bowl, mix flour and ½ cup sugar. Cut in butter, using pastry blender (or fork or pulling 2 table knives through mixture in opposite directions), until mixture looks like coarse crumbs.

4 Spoon filling mixture into crust-lined pie plate; sprinkle with streusel. Cover crust edge with foil to prevent excessive browning.

5 Bake 15 minutes. Reduce oven temperature to 375°F. Bake 30 minutes longer. Remove foil; bake 15 to 20 minutes longer or until browned and bubbly. Cool on cooling rack at least 3 hours before serving.

✱Two bags (16 oz each) frozen cut rhubarb, thawed and drained, can be substituted for the fresh rhubarb.

High Altitude (3500–6500 ft): After reducing temperature to 375°F, bake pie 30 minutes. Remove foil; continue baking 20 to 25 minutes longer or until browned and bubbly.

1 Serving: Calories 370; Total Fat 16g (Saturated Fat 8g; Trans Fat 0g); Cholesterol 25mg; Sodium 170mg; Total Carbohydrate 55g (Dietary Fiber 1g) **Exchanges:** ½ Starch, ½ Fruit, 2½ Other Carbohydrate, 3 Fat **Carbohydrate Choices:** 3½

 Pie Tip If you have a plentiful supply of fresh rhubarb, cut it into ½-inch pieces to make 5 cups, place in an airtight plastic freezer bag and freeze until ready to use. Just thaw and enjoy this rhubarb pie all year-round.

rhubarb-strawberry tart

Prep Time: 20 Minutes ✳ Start to Finish: 3 Hours 20 Minutes ✳ 12 servings

CRUST
1 Pillsbury refrigerated pie
   crust (from 15-oz box),
   softened as directed on box

FILLING
2 eggs

¾ cup granulated sugar

3 tablespoons all-purpose
   flour

¼ teaspoon almond extract

3 cups coarsely sliced fresh
   rhubarb*

2 cups sliced fresh
   strawberries

STREUSEL
½ cup packed brown sugar

¼ cup all-purpose flour

¼ teaspoon ground nutmeg

2 tablespoons cold butter or
   margarine, cut into pieces

1 Heat oven to 375°F. Place pie crust in 10-inch tart pan with removable bottom as directed on box for One-Crust Filled Pie. Trim edges if necessary.

2 In large bowl, beat eggs with electric mixer on medium speed until light. Beat in granulated sugar, 3 tablespoons flour and the almond extract until well blended. Alternately layer rhubarb and strawberries in crust-lined pan. Pour egg mixture over fruit.

3 In small bowl, mix brown sugar, ¼ cup flour and the nutmeg. Cut in butter, using pastry blender (or fork or pulling 2 table knives through mixture in opposite directions), until mixture looks like coarse crumbs. Sprinkle over top.

4 Bake 50 to 60 minutes or until crust is golden brown and filling is set in center. Cool completely on cooling rack, about 2 hours. To remove tart from sides of pan, place the pan on a wide, short can and pull down the side of the pan (see page 80). If necessary, use a thin-bladed knife to loosen crust from the side of the pan. Cut tart into wedges. Cover and refrigerate any remaining tart.

✱One bag (16 oz) frozen unsweetened rhubarb can be substituted for the fresh rhubarb. Increase bake time in step 4 to 55 to 65 minutes.

High Altitude (3500–6500 ft): In step 4, bake 53 to 57 minutes.

1 Serving: Calories 220; Total Fat 8g (Saturated Fat 3g; Trans Fat 0g); Cholesterol 45mg; Sodium 100mg; Total Carbohydrate 37g (Dietary Fiber 1g) **Exchanges:** 1 Starch, 1½ Other Carbohydrate, 1½ Fat **Carbohydrate Choices:** 2½

creamy and chilled favorites

Black-Bottom Banana Cream Pie, page 63

banana cream pie

Prep Time: 30 Minutes ✳ Start to Finish: 3 Hours 40 Minutes ✳ 8 servings

CRUST

1 Pillsbury refrigerated pie crust (from 15-oz box), softened as directed on box or Graham Cracker Crumb Crust (page 7)

FILLING

¾ cup sugar

¼ cup cornstarch

¼ teaspoon salt

3 cups milk

3 egg yolks, slightly beaten

2 tablespoons butter or margarine

2 teaspoons vanilla

2 to 3 medium bananas, sliced

TOPPING

Sweetened whipped cream or whipped topping, if desired

1 Heat oven to 450°F. Bake pie crust as directed on box for One-Crust Baked Shell, using 9-inch glass pie plate. Cool completely on cooling rack, about 15 minutes.

2 Meanwhile, in 2-quart saucepan, mix sugar, cornstarch and salt. Stir in milk until smooth. Cook over medium heat, stirring constantly, until mixture boils and thickens; boil and stir 2 minutes. Remove from heat.

3 Stir about ¼ cup hot mixture into egg yolks. Gradually stir yolk mixture into hot mixture. Cook over medium heat, stirring constantly, just until mixture begins to bubble and is thickened. Remove from heat; stir in butter and vanilla. Cool until lukewarm, about 20 minutes.

4 Arrange banana slices in cooled baked crust. Pour cooled pudding over bananas. Refrigerate until set, at least 3 hours. Top with whipped cream. Cover and refrigerate any remaining pie.

High Altitude (3500–6500 ft): In step 2, cook mixture over medium-high heat. In step 3, cook mixture over medium-high heat 2 minutes.

1 Serving: Calories 330; Total Fat 13g (Saturated Fat 6g; Trans Fat 0g); Cholesterol 95mg; Sodium 250mg; Total Carbohydrate 47g (Dietary Fiber 0g) **Exchanges:** 1½ Starch, ½ Fruit, 1 Other Carbohydrate, 2½ Fat **Carbohydrate Choices:** 3

coconut cream pie: Omit bananas. Stir in ¾ cup flaked coconut with the butter and vanilla. After topping pie with whipped cream, sprinkle with additional flaked coconut if desired.

black-bottom banana cream pie

Prep Time: 30 Minutes ❊ Start to Finish: 4 Hours 30 Minutes ❊ 8 servings

PUDDING

1 box (4-serving size) vanilla pudding and pie filling mix (not instant)

2 cups milk

CRUST

1 Pillsbury refrigerated pie crust (from 15-oz box), softened as directed on box

FILLING

1 cup whipping cream

²⁄₃ cup hot fudge topping

2 cups sliced ripe bananas (2 large bananas)

GARNISH

Chocolate curls, if desired

1 Make pudding mix with milk as directed on box for pie. Cool 30 minutes, stirring 2 or 3 times.

2 Meanwhile, heat oven to 450°F. Bake pie crust as directed on box for One-Crust Baked Shell, using 9-inch glass pie plate. Cool completely on cooling rack, about 15 minutes.

3 In chilled medium bowl, beat whipping cream with electric mixer on high speed until soft peaks form. Spread fudge topping evenly in bottom of cooled baked crust. Arrange banana slices on top of fudge. Spread pudding over bananas. Spread whipped cream over pudding. Refrigerate at least 4 hours until serving time. Garnish with chocolate curls. Cover and refrigerate any remaining pie.

High Altitude (3500–6500 ft): No change.

1 Serving: Calories 400; Total Fat 20g (Saturated Fat 10g; Trans Fat 0g); Cholesterol 40mg; Sodium 300mg; Total Carbohydrate 51g (Dietary Fiber 1g) **Exchanges:** 1 Starch, ½ Fruit, 2 Other Carbohydrate, 4 Fat **Carbohydrate Choices:** 3½

See photo on page 61.

Pie Tip To make chocolate curls, warm a chocolate bar by holding it in your hands for several minutes. Run a vegetable peeler across the bar to create the curls. (See photo on page 61.)

apricot-coconut cream pie

Harriet Warkentin | San Jacinto, CA | Bake-Off® Contest 33, 1988

Prep Time: 30 Minutes ✳ Start to Finish: 5 Hours 15 Minutes ✳ 8 servings

CRUST

1 Pillsbury refrigerated pie crust (from 15-oz box), softened as directed on box

FILLING

1 envelope unflavored gelatin

1 cup apricot nectar

2 cans (16 oz each) apricot halves, drained

½ cup sugar

¼ cup cornstarch

¼ teaspoon salt

1¾ cups milk

4 egg yolks, beaten

1 tablespoon butter or margarine

½ teaspoon vanilla

½ cup coconut, toasted

TOPPING

1 cup whipping cream

1 tablespoon sugar

¼ teaspoon vanilla

2 to 3 tablespoons apricot preserves, melted

½ cup coconut, toasted

1 Heat oven to 450°F. Bake pie crust as directed on box for One-Crust Baked Shell, using 9-inch glass pie plate. Cool completely on cooling rack, about 15 minutes.

2 Meanwhile, in small bowl, sprinkle gelatin over ¼ cup of the apricot nectar; let stand to soften. Set aside. In another small bowl, cut 1 can of the apricot halves into small pieces. Set aside. In blender or food processor, place remaining can apricot halves and remaining ¾ cup apricot nectar. Cover; blend or process until smooth.

3 In 2-quart saucepan, mix ½ cup sugar, the cornstarch and salt. Stir in milk and blended apricot mixture. (Mixture will look curdled.) Cook over medium heat, stirring constantly, until mixture heats to boiling and is slightly thickened. Boil 2 minutes, stirring constantly. Remove from heat. Blend a small amount of hot mixture into egg yolks. Return egg yolk mixture to saucepan; mix well. Over medium heat, heat to boiling, stirring constantly. Boil 2 minutes, stirring constantly.

4 Remove from heat; stir in butter, ½ teaspoon vanilla and the gelatin mixture. Fold in ½ cup toasted coconut. Refrigerate about 30 minutes or until slightly thickened. Fold in apricot pieces. Spoon into cooled baked crust. Cover; refrigerate about 45 minutes or until mixture is partially set.

5 In chilled large bowl, beat whipping cream with electric mixer on high speed until soft peaks form. Add 1 tablespoon sugar and ¼ teaspoon vanilla; beat until stiff peaks form. Gently fold in apricot preserves. Pipe or spoon whipped cream mixture over cooled filling. Garnish with remaining ½ cup toasted coconut. Refrigerate 3 to 4 hours or until set. Cover and refrigerate any remaining pie.

High Altitude (3500–6500 ft): No change.

1 Serving: Calories 460; Total Fat 24g (Saturated Fat 14g; Trans Fat 0g); Cholesterol 145mg; Sodium 260mg; Total Carbohydrate 55g (Dietary Fiber 2g) **Exchanges:** ½ Starch, 3 Other Carbohydrate, ½ High-Fat Meat, 4 Fat **Carbohydrate Choices:** 3½

Pie Tip To toast coconut, spread in a thin layer on a cookie sheet. Bake at 375°F about 5 minutes or until light golden brown. Or, spread in a thin layer in a microwavable glass pie plate. Microwave on Medium 4½ to 8 minutes or until light golden brown, tossing with a fork after each minute.

banana split tart

Prep Time: 20 Minutes ✳ Start to Finish: 1 Hour 15 Minutes ✳ 16 servings

CRUST

1 box (15 oz) Pillsbury refrigerated pie crusts, softened as directed on box

FILLING

½ cup semisweet chocolate chips, melted

2 containers (6 oz each) banana crème low-fat yogurt

2 small bananas, sliced

1 can (21 oz) strawberry pie filling with more fruit

1 cup sliced fresh strawberries

1 Heat oven to 375°F. On ungreased large cookie sheet, unroll 1 pie crust. Unroll second pie crust and place over first crust, matching edges and pressing to seal. With rolling pin, roll into 14-inch round.

2 Fold ½ inch of crust edge under, forming border; press to seal seam. Flute edge if desired. Prick crust generously with fork.

3 Bake 20 to 25 minutes or until golden brown. Cool completely on cooling rack, about 30 minutes.

4 Spread ¼ cup of the melted chocolate chips evenly over cooled baked crust. Spread yogurt evenly over chocolate. Arrange banana slices on top of yogurt. Spread pie filling evenly over top. Arrange strawberries over pie filling. Drizzle remaining melted chocolate over top. Cut into wedges and serve. Cover and refrigerate any remaining tart.

High Altitude (3500–6500 ft): No change.

1 Serving: Calories 280; Total Fat 9g (Saturated Fat 3.5g; Trans Fat 0g); Cholesterol 0mg; Sodium 135mg; Total Carbohydrate 50g (Dietary Fiber 1g) **Exchanges:** ½ Starch, 2½ Other Carbohydrate, 2 Fat **Carbohydrate Choices:** 3

Pie Tip To make this a "real" banana split treat, top each serving with a dollop of whipped topping and a sprinkle of chopped nuts.

blueberry-lemon tart

Prep Time: 20 Minutes ✳ Start to Finish: 1 Hour 15 Minutes ✳ 16 servings

CRUST

1 box (15 oz) Pillsbury refrigerated pie crusts, softened as directed on box

FILLING

2 containers (6 oz each) lemon burst low-fat yogurt

1 package (8 oz) cream cheese, softened

1 can (21 oz) blueberry pie filling with more fruit

1 cup fresh blueberries

1 Heat oven to 375°F. On ungreased large cookie sheet, unroll 1 pie crust. Unroll second pie crust and place over first crust, matching edges and pressing to seal. With rolling pin, roll out into 14-inch round.

2 Fold ½ inch of crust edge under, forming border; press to seal seam. Flute edge if desired. Prick crust generously with fork.

3 Bake 20 to 25 minutes or until golden brown. Cool completely on cooling rack, about 30 minutes.

4 In medium bowl, beat yogurt and cream cheese with electric mixer on medium speed until blended. Spread evenly over cooled baked crust. Spread pie filling evenly over yogurt mixture. Top with blueberries. Cut into wedges to serve. Cover and refrigerate any remaining tart.

High Altitude (3500–6500 ft): In step 3, bake 17 to 22 minutes.

1 Serving: Calories 230; Total Fat 12g (Saturated Fat 6g; Trans Fat 0g); Cholesterol 20mg; Sodium 160mg; Total Carbohydrate 29g (Dietary Fiber 0g) **Exchanges:** ½ Starch, 1½ Other Carbohydrate, 2½ Fat **Carbohydrate Choices:** 2

blueberry-lime tart: Substitute 2 containers (6 oz each) Key lime pie low-fat yogurt for the lemon burst.

raspberry-lemon tart: Substitute 1 can (21 oz) raspberry pie filling with more fruit for the blueberry pie filling and 1 cup fresh raspberries for the blueberries.

chai cream pie

Prep Time: 25 Minutes ✱ Start to Finish: 2 Hours 50 Minutes ✱ 8 servings

CRUST

1 Pillsbury refrigerated pie
crust (from 15-oz box),
softened as directed on box
or Vanilla Cookie Crumb
Crust (page 7)

FILLING

1 cup water

1 package (1.1 oz) chai tea
latte mix

1 bag (10.5 oz) miniature
marshmallows (6 cups)

1 tablespoon butter or
margarine

2 tablespoons caramel-
flavored sundae syrup

1½ cups whipping cream

¼ cup chopped pecans

Shaved chocolate

1 Heat oven to 450°F. Bake pie crust as directed on box for One-Crust Baked Shell, using 9-inch glass pie plate. Cool completely on cooling rack, about 15 minutes.

2 Meanwhile, in 3-quart saucepan, heat water to boiling over high heat. Stir in chai mix; reduce heat to low. Using whisk, stir in marshmallows and butter. Continue stirring just until marshmallows are melted. Stir in caramel syrup. Refrigerate about 30 minutes or until cool and thickened.

3 In chilled medium bowl, beat whipping cream with electric mixer on high speed until stiff peaks form. Set aside 1 cup whipped cream. Fold remaining whipped cream into cooled filling. Pour into cooled baked crust. Sprinkle with pecans. Cover; refrigerate about 2 hours or until filling is set. Garnish with reserved 1 cup whipped cream and the shaved chocolate. Cover and refrigerate any remaining pie.

High Altitude (3500–6500 ft): No change.

1 Serving: Calories 440; Total Fat 25g (Saturated Fat 12g; Trans Fat 0.5g); Cholesterol 60mg; Sodium 210mg; Total Carbohydrate 51g (Dietary Fiber 0g) **Exchanges:** ½ Starch, 3 Other Carbohydrate, 5 Fat **Carbohydrate Choices:** 3½

Pie Tip Chai tea mix comes in an assortment of flavors. This recipe was created using a black tea, honey, vanilla and spices blend.

french silk chocolate pie

Betty Cooper | Kensington, MD | Bake-Off® Contest 03, 1951

Prep Time: 50 Minutes ✳ Start to Finish: 2 Hours 50 Minutes ✳ 10 servings

CRUST
1 Pillsbury refrigerated pie crust (from 15-oz box), softened as directed on box

FILLING
3 oz unsweetened baking chocolate, cut into pieces

1 cup butter, softened (do not use margarine)

1 cup sugar

½ teaspoon vanilla

4 pasteurized eggs* or 1 cup fat-free egg product

TOPPING
½ cup sweetened whipped cream

Chocolate curls, if desired

1 Heat oven to 450°F. Bake pie crust as directed on box for One-Crust Baked Shell, using 9-inch glass pie plate. Cool completely on cooling rack, about 15 minutes.

2 In 1-quart saucepan, melt chocolate over low heat; cool. In small bowl, beat butter with electric mixer on medium speed until fluffy. Gradually add sugar, beating until light and fluffy. Add cooled chocolate and vanilla; beat well.

3 Add eggs 1 at a time, beating on high speed 2 minutes after each addition. Beat until mixture is smooth and fluffy. Pour into cooled baked crust. Refrigerate at least 2 hours before serving, or until set. Top with whipped cream and chocolate curls. Cover and refrigerate any remaining pie.

✳Pasteurized eggs are uncooked eggs that have been heat-treated to kill bacteria. Because the eggs in this recipe are not cooked, be sure to use pasteurized eggs. They can be found in the dairy case at large supermarkets.

High Altitude (3500–6500 ft): No change.

1 Serving: Calories 460; Total Fat 34g (Saturated Fat 19g; Trans Fat 1g); Cholesterol 150mg; Sodium 250mg; Total Carbohydrate 34g (Dietary Fiber 1g) **Exchanges:** 1 Starch, 1½ Other Carbohydrate, 6½ Fat **Carbohydrate Choices:** 2

 Margarine is not recommended for the filling. If you use margarine, the filling will look curdled, and it will not be as creamy and smooth. Butter also adds to the rich flavor of this delectable prize-winning pie.

chocolate raspberry mousse pie

Prep Time: 1 Hour * Start to Finish: 5 Hours * 8 servings

CRUST
1 Pillsbury refrigerated pie
  crust (from 15-oz box),
  softened as directed on box

FILLING
⅓ cup whipping cream

½ cup semisweet chocolate
  chips

2 boxes (10 oz each) frozen
  raspberries in syrup, thawed

1 envelope unflavored gelatin

1½ cups whipping cream

⅓ cup powdered sugar

TOPPING
½ cup whipping cream

1 cup fresh raspberries

1 Heat oven to 450°F. Bake pie crust as directed on box for One-Crust Baked Shell, using 9-inch glass pie plate. Cool completely on cooling rack, about 15 minutes.

2 In 1-quart saucepan, heat ⅓ cup whipping cream just to boiling. Remove from heat. Add chocolate chips; stir until melted. Pour into cooled baked crust. Cool completely.

3 Meanwhile, in food processor bowl with metal blade, process thawed raspberries in syrup until smooth. Place strainer over 2-quart saucepan; pour pureed raspberries into strainer. Press raspberries with back of spoon through strainer to remove seeds; discard seeds. Sprinkle gelatin over raspberries in saucepan; let stand 1 minute to soften.

4 Cook raspberry mixture over medium heat until gelatin is completely dissolved, stirring frequently. Cover; refrigerate 2 to 3 hours, stirring occasionally, until mixture mounds slightly when dropped from spoon.

5 In large bowl, beat 1½ cups whipping cream and the powdered sugar with electric mixer on high speed until stiff peaks form. Gently fold raspberry mixture into whipped cream. Spoon over chocolate in cooled baked crust. Refrigerate until set, about 2 hours.

6 In chilled medium bowl, beat ½ cup whipping cream with electric mixer on high speed until soft peaks form. Serve pie with whipped cream and fresh raspberries. Cover and refrigerator any remaining pie and whipped cream.

High Altitude (3500–6500 ft): No change.

1 Serving: Calories 600; Total Fat 39g (Saturated Fat 20g; Trans Fat 1g); Cholesterol 85mg; Sodium 250mg; Total Carbohydrate 60g (Dietary Fiber 4g) **Exchanges:** 1 Starch, 1 Fruit, 2 Other Carbohydrate, 7½ Fat **Carbohydrate Choices:** 4

Pie Tip After sprinkling the gelatin on the raspberry mixture, it is important to let it stand a minute or two. This softens and swells the gelatin granules so they dissolve completely when heated.

white and dark chocolate raspberry tart

Prep Time: 1 Hour 5 Minutes ✳ Start to Finish: 4 Hours 50 Minutes ✳ 10 servings

CRUST

1 Pillsbury refrigerated pie crust (from 15-oz box), softened as directed on box

FILLING

2 tablespoons orange juice

1 teaspoon unflavored gelatin

1½ cups whipping cream

1 package (6 oz) white chocolate baking bars, chopped

1 bag (10 or 12 oz) frozen whole raspberries, thawed, juice reserved

1 tablespoon cornstarch

1 tablespoon sugar

1 cup fresh raspberries

2 oz semisweet baking chocolate, cut into pieces

2 tablespoons butter or margarine

GARNISH, IF DESIRED

White chocolate curls

Additional raspberries

1 Heat oven to 450°F. Bake pie crust as directed on box for One-Crust Baked Shell, using 10-inch tart pan with removable bottom or 10-inch springform pan, and pressing 1 inch up side of pan. Cool completely on cooling rack, about 15 minutes.

2 in 2-quart saucepan, place orange juice. Sprinkle gelatin over juice; let stand 5 minutes to soften. Stir in ¾ cup of the whipping cream; heat over low heat, stirring frequently, until gelatin is dissolved. Stir in chopped white chocolate until melted and smooth. Transfer to medium bowl; refrigerate about 30 minutes, stirring occasionally, until cool but not set.

3 In blender or food processor, place thawed raspberries and any juice. Cover; blend until pureed. Set strainer over 2-cup measuring cup. Press puree with back of spoon through strainer to remove seeds. Discard seeds. If necessary, add water to raspberry puree to measure ½ cup. In 1-quart saucepan, mix cornstarch and 1 tablespoon sugar. Gradually add raspberry puree. Cook over low heat, stirring constantly, until thickened. Fold in fresh raspberries; spread evenly over cooled baked crust. Refrigerate 15 minutes.

4 Meanwhile, in chilled large bowl, beat remaining ¾ cup whipping cream with electric mixer on high speed until stiff peaks form. Fold whipped cream into white chocolate mixture. Spoon and spread over raspberry layer. Refrigerate about 1 hour or until filling is set.

5 In 1-quart saucepan, melt semisweet chocolate and butter over low heat, stirring frequently; carefully pour and spread evenly over white chocolate layer. Refrigerate at least 2 hours or until set. To serve, let stand at room temperature about 30 minutes to soften chocolate layers. Garnish with chocolate curls and additional raspberries. To remove tart from sides of pan, place the pan on a wide, short can and pull down the side of the pan (see page 80). If necessary, use a thin-bladed knife to loosen crust from the side of the pan. Cover and refrigerate any remaining tart.

High Altitude (3500–6500 ft): No change.

1 Serving: Calories 390; Total Fat 27g (Saturated Fat 16g; Trans Fat 0g); Cholesterol 50mg; Sodium 135mg; Total Carbohydrate 33g (Dietary Fiber 2g) **Exchanges:** 1 Starch, 1 Other Carbohydrate, 5½ Fat **Carbohydrate Choices:** 2

chocolate-strawberry pie

Prep Time: 30 Minutes ✷ Start to Finish: 2 Hours 30 Minutes ✷ 8 servings

CRUST

1 Pillsbury refrigerated pie crust (from 15-oz box), softened as directed on box

FILLING

1 cup semisweet chocolate chips (6 oz)

2 tablespoons butter or margarine

¼ cup powdered sugar

3 tablespoons kirsch or water

1 package (8 oz) cream cheese, softened

1½ to 2 pints (3 to 4 cups) fresh strawberries, halved

GLAZE

3 tablespoons red currant jelly

2 teaspoons kirsch or water

1 Heat oven to 450°F. Bake pie crust as directed on box for One-Crust Baked Shell, using 10-inch tart pan with removable bottom or 9-inch glass pie plate. Cool completely on cooling rack, about 15 minutes.

2 In 2-quart saucepan, melt chocolate chips and butter over low heat, stirring constantly. Stir in powdered sugar, 3 tablespoons kirsch and the cream cheese until well blended. Pour into cooled baked crust. Arrange strawberries over chocolate mixture.

3 In 1-quart saucepan, heat jelly with 2 teaspoons kirsch until warm; spoon or brush over strawberries. Refrigerate at least 2 hours until chilled. To remove tart from sides of pan, place the pan on a wide, short can and pull down the side of the pan (see page 80). If necessary, use a thin-bladed knife to loosen crust from the side of the pan. Cover and refrigerate any remaining pie.

High Altitude (3500–6500 ft): No change.

1 Serving: Calories 420; Total Fat 26g (Saturated Fat 14g; Trans Fat 0g); Cholesterol 45mg; Sodium 220mg; Total Carbohydrate 41g (Dietary Fiber 2g) **Exchanges:** 2½ Other Carbohydrate, ½ High-Fat Meat, 4½ Fat **Carbohydrate Choices:** 3

 Pie Tip Rather than making the glaze, use purchased strawberry glaze, usually found next to fresh strawberries in the produce section of your local supermarket.

black forest tart

Prep Time: 30 Minutes ✳ Start to Finish: 2 Hours ✳ 12 servings

CRUST

1 Pillsbury refrigerated pie crust (from 15-oz box), softened as directed on box

FILLING

6 oz semisweet baking chocolate, cut into pieces

2 tablespoons butter or margarine

¼ cup powdered sugar

1 package (8 oz) cream cheese, softened

1 can (21 oz) cherry pie filling with more fruit

TOPPING

1 cup whipping cream

1 oz semisweet baking chocolate, grated

1 Heat oven to 450°F. Place pie crust in 9-inch glass pie plate or 10-inch tart pan with removable bottom as directed on box for One-Crust Filled Pie. Bake 10 to 12 minutes or until lightly browned. Cool completely on cooling rack, about 15 minutes.

2 Meanwhile, in 1-quart saucepan, melt 6 oz chocolate and the butter over low heat, stirring constantly; remove from heat. In small bowl, beat powdered sugar and cream cheese with electric mixer on medium speed until smooth. Stir in melted chocolate mixture; beat until smooth. Add 1 cup of the cherry pie filling; blend gently with a spoon. Set aside remaining pie filling. Spread mixture evenly in cooled baked crust. Refrigerate 1 hour.

3 In chilled medium bowl, beat whipping cream with electric mixer on high speed until soft peaks form. Gently fold in the grated chocolate. Spread evenly over cooled chocolate layer. Spoon remaining cherry pie filling around outer edge of tart. Refrigerate until serving time. Cover and refrigerate any remaining tart.

High Altitude (3500–6500 ft): No change.

1 Serving: Calories 370; Total Fat 24g (Saturated Fat 14g; Trans Fat 0g); Cholesterol 50mg; Sodium 150mg; Total Carbohydrate 35g (Dietary Fiber 2g) **Exchanges:** 1 Starch, 1½ Other Carbohydrate, 4½ Fat **Carbohydrate Choices:** 2

 This impressive chocolate-cherry tart is great for entertaining. It can be made up to 24 hours ahead of time and stored covered in the refrigerator. Instead of using the grated chocolate in the whipped cream, spread the tart with whipped cream. Spoon the remaining cherry pie filling around the edge, and fill the center with large chocolate curls.

coffee crunch chocolate tart

Vesta Frizzel | Independence, MO | Bake-Off® Contest 32, 1986

Prep Time: 25 Minutes ✳ Start to Finish: 2 Hours 55 Minutes ✳ 12 servings

CRUST

1 Pillsbury refrigerated pie crust (from 15-oz box), softened as directed on box

CRUMB LAYER

½ cup crisp coconut cookie crumbs (3 to 4 cookies)

2 tablespoons all-purpose flour

2 tablespoons packed brown sugar

1 to 2 teaspoons instant coffee granules or crystals

1 tablespoon butter or margarine

FILLING

1 cup powdered sugar

1 package (3 oz) cream cheese, softened

1½ teaspoons vanilla

2 oz unsweetened baking chocolate, melted

2 cups whipping cream

GARNISH, IF DESIRED

Unsweetened baking cocoa

Chocolate-coated coffee beans

1 Heat oven to 450°F. Place pie crust in 10-inch tart pan with removable bottom or 9-inch glass pie plate; press in bottom and up side of pan. Trim edges if necessary. Generously prick crust with fork.

2 In small bowl, mix cookie crumbs, flour, brown sugar and instant coffee. Cut in butter, using pastry blender (or fork or pulling 2 table knives through mixture in opposite directions), until mixture looks like coarse crumbs. Sprinkle over bottom of crust-lined pan. Bake 12 to 16 minutes or until light golden brown. Cool completely on cooling rack, about 30 minutes.

3 In large bowl, beat powdered sugar, cream cheese and vanilla with electric mixer on high speed until well blended. Add chocolate; beat until smooth. Gradually add whipping cream, beating until stiff peaks form. Spread filling evenly in cooled baked crust. Refrigerate 2 to 3 hours. To remove tart from sides of pan, place the pan on a wide, short can and pull down the side of the pan (see page 80). If necessary, use a thin-bladed knife to loosen crust from the side of the pan. Sprinkle with baking cocoa, and garnish with chocolate-coated coffee beans. Cover and refrigerate any remaining tart.

High Altitude (3500–6500 ft): No change.

1 Serving: Calories 330; Total Fat 23g (Saturated Fat 14g; Trans Fat 0.5g); Cholesterol 55mg; Sodium 125mg; Total Carbohydrate 26g (Dietary Fiber 0g) **Exchanges:** 1½ Other Carbohydrate, ½ High-Fat Meat, 4 Fat **Carbohydrate Choices:** 2

Pie Tip If you have extra coconut cookies, crush them and sprinkle over the top of the tart instead of the cocoa and chocolate-coated coffee beans.

chocolate-nut truffle pie

Prep Time: 30 Minutes ✳ Start to Finish: 4 Hours 30 Minutes ✳ 12 servings

CRUST

1 Pillsbury refrigerated pie
   crust (from 15-oz box),
   softened as directed on box

¼ cup finely chopped pecans

FILLING

12 oz semisweet baking
    chocolate, coarsely chopped

2 cups whipping cream

TOPPING

½ cup whipping cream

12 pecan halves

1 Heat oven to 450°F. Bake pie crust as directed on box for One-Crust Baked Shell, using 9-inch glass pie plate—except before baking, sprinkle chopped pecans over bottom of crust; lightly press into crust. Cool completely on cooling rack, about 15 minutes.

2 Meanwhile, in large bowl, place chocolate. In 2-quart saucepan, heat 2 cups whipping cream over medium heat just until it begins to boil. Pour over chocolate. With electric mixer on low speed, beat about 1 minute or until chocolate mixture is smooth. Pour into cooled baked crust. Refrigerate at least 4 hours until serving time.

3 In chilled small bowl, beat ½ cup whipping cream with electric mixer on high speed until stiff peaks form. Spoon or pipe whipped cream around outer edge of pie. Garnish with pecan halves. Cover and refrigerate any remaining pie.

High Altitude (3500–6500 ft): No change.

1 Serving: Calories 410; Total Fat 31g (Saturated Fat 17g; Trans Fat 0.5g); Cholesterol 60mg; Sodium 95mg; Total Carbohydrate 29g (Dietary Fiber 2g) **Exchanges:** 1 Starch, 1 Other Carbohydrate, 6 Fat **Carbohydrate Choices:** 2

 Pie Tip To make this luscious chocolate pie, be sure to use squares of baking chocolate for the filling. Chocolate chips will not produce the same smooth filling, and it will be slightly grainy.

mixed fresh berry tart

Prep Time: 15 Minutes ✳ Start to Finish: 2 Hours 30 Minutes ✳ 8 servings

CRUST

1 Pillsbury refrigerated pie crust (from 15-oz box), softened as directed on box

FILLING

1 package (8 oz) cream cheese, softened

⅓ cup sugar

1 tablespoon orange-flavored liqueur or orange juice

4 cups assorted fresh whole berries (such as small strawberries, blueberries, raspberries, and/or blackberries)

⅓ cup red currant jelly, melted

1 Heat oven to 450°F. Bake pie crust as directed on box for One-Crust Baked Shell, using 9-inch tart pan with removable bottom. Cool completely on cooling rack, about 15 minutes.

2 In small bowl, beat cream cheese, sugar and liqueur with electric mixer on medium speed until well blended and smooth. Spread mixture evenly in cooled baked crust.

3 Arrange berries on top of cream cheese mixture. Brush berries with melted jelly to glaze. Refrigerate at least 2 hours before serving. To remove tart from sides of pan, place the pan on a wide, short can and pull down the side of the pan (see photo). If necessary, use a thin-bladed knife to loosen crust from the side of the pan. Cover and refrigerate any remaining tart.

High Altitude (3500–6500 ft): No change.

1 Serving: Calories 330; Total Fat 17g (Saturated Fat 9g; Trans Fat 0g); Cholesterol 35mg; Sodium 200mg; Total Carbohydrate 40g (Dietary Fiber 3g) **Exchanges:** 1 Starch, ½ Fruit, 1 Other Carbohydrate, 3½ Fat **Carbohydrate Choices:** 2½

Pie Tip This luscious berry tart is great for entertaining because the crust and cream cheese filling can be assembled and refrigerated up to 12 hours before serving. Just before serving, arrange the berries over the tart and brush with the melted jelly.

Removing Tart From Pan

To remove a tart from the pan, place the pan on a wide, short can and pull down the side of the pan. If you don't have a can, hold the tart in both hands and push the bottom up and let the side of the pan slip onto your arm.

elegant fruit tart

Prep Time: 15 Minutes ✳ Start to Finish: 50 Minutes ✳ 10 servings

CRUST

1 Pillsbury refrigerated pie crust (from 15-oz box), softened as directed on box

FILLING

1 package (8 oz) cream cheese, softened

2 tablespoons milk

¼ cup powdered sugar

½ teaspoon grated orange peel

2 to 3 cups assorted cut-up fresh fruit (strawberries, blueberries, raspberries, peaches, kiwifruit, grapes)

1 Heat oven to 450°F. On ungreased cookie sheet, unroll pie crust. Flute edge, if desired. Generously prick crust with fork. Bake 9 to 11 minutes or until lightly browned. Cool completely on cooling rack, about 30 minutes.

2 In small bowl, beat cream cheese, milk, powdered sugar and orange peel with electric mixer on medium speed until smooth. Place cooled baked crust on serving plate; spread evenly with cream cheese mixture to within ½ inch of edge. Arrange fruit on cream cheese mixture. Cover and refrigerate any remaining tart.

High Altitude (3500–6500 ft): No change.

1 Serving: Calories 290; Total Fat 19g (Saturated Fat 9g; Trans Fat 0g); Cholesterol 30mg; Sodium 240mg; Total Carbohydrate 27g (Dietary Fiber 0g) **Exchanges:** 1 Starch, ½ Other Carbohydrate, 4 Fat **Carbohydrate Choices:** 2

elegant strawberry tart: Add ½ cup sliced small strawberries to the cream cheese mixture; beat with electric mixer on medium speed until blended. Spread strawberry mixture evenly on baked crust; arrange 3 cups small strawberries, halved (instead of assorted fruit) on the cream cheese mixture.

Pie Tip Using melted jelly to glaze fruit tarts is a bakery secret. Melt ⅓ cup apple or red currant jelly, or apricot or peach preserves, and brush it over the fruit.

lemon cream cheese–blueberry pie

Prep Time: 20 Minutes ✳ Start to Finish: 1 Hour 35 Minutes ✳ 8 servings

CRUST

1 Pillsbury refrigerated pie crust (from 15-oz box), softened as directed on box

FILLING

1 package (8 oz) cream cheese, softened

1½ cups milk

1 box (4-serving size) lemon instant pudding and pie filling mix

TOPPING

1 can (21 oz) blueberry pie filling with more fruit

1 cup frozen (thawed) whipped topping

Lemon peel, if desired

1 Heat oven to 450°F. Bake pie crust as directed on box for One-Crust Baked Shell, using 9-inch glass pie plate. Cool completely on cooling rack, about 15 minutes.

2 Meanwhile, in small bowl, beat cream cheese with electric mixer on medium speed until fluffy. In medium bowl, beat milk and pudding mix with electric mixer on medium speed until well blended. Add cream cheese; beat until smooth.

3 Spread cream cheese–pudding mixture evenly in cooled baked crust. Refrigerate 1 hour. Top individual servings with blueberry pie filling; garnish with whipped topping and lemon peel. Cover and refrigerate any remaining pie.

High Altitude (3500–6500 ft): No change.

1 Serving: Calories 390; Total Fat 20g (Saturated Fat 11g; Trans Fat 0g); Cholesterol 40mg; Sodium 390mg; Total Carbohydrate 50g (Dietary Fiber 0g) **Exchanges:** 3½ Other Carbohydrate, ½ High-Fat Meat, 3 Fat **Carbohydrate Choices:** 3

chocolate cream cheese–cherry pie: Substitute chocolate instant pudding for the lemon, and cherry pie filling for the blueberry. Garnish with chocolate curls.

butterscotch cream cheese–apple pie: Substitute butterscotch instant pudding for the lemon, and apple pie filling for the blueberry. Garnish with fresh apple pieces.

Pie Tip After spreading the filling in the baked crust, you can cover and refrigerate it up to 12 hours. Just before serving, top each piece with the blueberry pie filling and whipped topping.

lemon truffle pie

Patricia Kiewiet | LaGrange, IL | Bake-Off® Contest 35, 1992

Prep Time: 45 Minutes ✻ Start to Finish: 3 Hours 45 Minutes ✻ 10 servings

CRUST

1 Pillsbury refrigerated pie crust (from 15-oz box), softened as directed on box

LEMON LAYER

1 cup sugar

2 tablespoons cornstarch

2 tablespoons all-purpose flour

1 cup water

2 egg yolks, beaten

1 tablespoon butter or margarine

½ teaspoon grated lemon peel

¼ cup lemon juice

CREAM CHEESE LAYER

1 cup white vanilla baking chips or chopped white chocolate baking bar (6 oz)

1 package (8 oz) ⅓-less-fat cream cheese (Neufchâtel), softened

TOPPING

½ cup whipping cream

1 tablespoon sliced almonds, toasted

1 Heat oven to 450°F. Bake pie crust as directed on box for One-Crust Baked Shell, using 9-inch glass pie plate. Cool completely on cooling rack, about 15 minutes.

2 Meanwhile, in 2-quart saucepan, mix sugar, cornstarch and flour. Gradually stir in water until smooth. Heat to boiling over medium heat, stirring constantly. Reduce heat to low; cook 2 minutes, stirring constantly. Remove from heat. Stir about ¼ cup hot mixture into egg yolks until well blended. Stir egg yolk mixture into mixture in saucepan. Heat to boiling over low heat, stirring constantly. Cook 2 minutes, stirring constantly. Remove from heat. Stir in butter, lemon peel and lemon juice.

3 In 1-quart saucepan, place ⅓ cup hot lemon mixture; cool remaining lemon mixture 15 minutes. Into hot mixture in saucepan, stir vanilla baking chips. Cook and stir over low heat just until chips are melted.

4 In small bowl, beat cream cheese with electric mixer on medium speed until fluffy. Beat in melted vanilla chip mixture until well blended. Spread mixture evenly in bottom of cooled baked crust. Spoon lemon mixture evenly over cream cheese layer. Refrigerate until set, 2 to 3 hours.

5 Just before serving, in chilled small bowl, beat whipping cream with electric mixer on high speed until stiff peaks form. Pipe or spoon whipped cream over pie. Garnish with toasted almonds. Cover and refrigerate any remaining pie.

High Altitude (3500–6500 ft): No change.

1 Serving: Calories 430; Total Fat 23g (Saturated Fat 14g; Trans Fat 0g); Cholesterol 75mg; Sodium 240mg; Total Carbohydrate 49g (Dietary Fiber 0g) **Exchanges:** ½ Starch, 3 Other Carbohydrate, ½ High-Fat Meat, 3½ Fat **Carbohydrate Choices:** 3

Pie Tip To toast almonds, heat oven to 350°F. Spread almonds in ungreased shallow pan. Bake uncovered 6 to 10 minutes, stirring occasionally, until light brown. Or sprinkle in ungreased heavy skillet. Cook over medium heat 5 to 7 minutes, stirring frequently, until almonds begin to brown, then stirring constantly until light brown.

lemon meringue pie

Prep Time: 55 Minutes ✳ Start to Finish: 5 Hours 40 Minutes ✳ 8 servings

CRUST

1 Pillsbury refrigerated pie crust (from 15-oz box), softened as directed on box

FILLING

1¼ cups sugar

⅓ cup cornstarch

½ teaspoon salt

1½ cups cold water

3 egg yolks

2 tablespoons butter or margarine

1 tablespoon grated lemon peel

½ cup fresh lemon juice

MERINGUE

3 egg whites

¼ teaspoon cream of tartar

½ teaspoon vanilla

¼ cup sugar

1 Heat oven to 450°F. Bake pie crust as directed on box for One-Crust Baked Shell, using 9-inch glass pie plate. Cool completely on cooling rack, about 15 minutes.

2 Meanwhile, in 2-quart saucepan, mix 1¼ cups sugar, the cornstarch and salt. Gradually stir in cold water until smooth. Cook over medium heat, stirring constantly, until mixture boils; boil 1 minute, stirring constantly. Remove from heat.

3 In small bowl, beat egg yolks with whisk. Stir about ¼ cup of hot mixture into egg yolks. Gradually stir yolk mixture into hot mixture. Cook over low heat, stirring constantly, until mixture boils; boil 1 minute, stirring constantly. Remove from heat. Stir in butter, lemon peel and lemon juice. Cool slightly, about 15 minutes.

4 Reduce oven temperature to 350°F. Pour filling into cooled baked crust. In small deep bowl, beat egg whites, cream of tartar and vanilla with electric mixer on medium speed about 1 minute or until soft peaks form. On high speed, beat in ¼ cup sugar, 1 tablespoon at a time, until stiff glossy peaks form and sugar is dissolved. Spoon meringue onto hot filling, spreading evenly to edge of crust to seal well and prevent shrinkage.

5 Bake at 350°F 12 to 15 minutes or until meringue is light golden brown. Cool completely on cooling rack, about 1 hour. Refrigerate until filling is set, about 3 hours. Cover and refrigerate any remaining pie.

High Altitude (3500–6500 ft): In step 5, bake about 20 minutes or until meringue is light golden brown.

1 Serving: Calories 360; Total Fat 14g (Saturated Fat 4g; Trans Fat 1.5g); Cholesterol 85mg; Sodium 340mg; Total Carbohydrate 56g (Dietary Fiber 0g) **Exchanges:** 1½ Starch, 2 Other Carbohydrate, 2½ Fat **Carbohydrate Choices:** 4

Pie Tip For perfect meringue, have the egg whites at room temperature, add the sugar very slowly and beat the egg whites until stiff but still glossy. Swirl the meringue in soft mounds on top of the filling, not in peaks. Peaks can overbrown before the meringue is baked.

individual lemon-lime cream tarts

Prep Time: 30 Minutes ✳ Start to Finish: 45 Minutes ✳ 4 tarts

CRUST
1 Pillsbury refrigerated pie
   crust (from 15-oz box),
   softened as directed on box

FILLING
1 package (3 oz) cream cheese,
   softened

2 tablespoons powdered sugar

2 tablespoons whipping cream

1 teaspoon grated lime peel

¼ cup lemon curd (from
   10-oz jar)

GARNISH
Whipped cream

Strips of lime peel

Strips of lemon peel

1 Heat oven to 450°F. Unroll pie crust on work surface. Use 4-inch round cutter to cut four 4-inch rounds from crust. Press each round into 4-inch tart pan; prick bottom of each with fork. Bake 5 to 9 minutes or until golden brown. Cool completely on cooling rack, about 15 minutes.

2 Meanwhile, in small bowl, beat cream cheese, powdered sugar and whipping cream with electric mixer on medium speed until smooth. Divide evenly among cooled tart shells.

3 In small bowl, mix grated lime peel into lemon curd until smooth. Spoon evenly over cream cheese mixture in shells to within ¼ inch of edges. Garnish with whipped cream and strips of lime and lemon peel.

High Altitude (3500–6500 ft): No change.

1 Tart: Calories 290; Total Fat 18g (Saturated Fat 9g; Trans Fat 0g); Cholesterol 50mg; Sodium 190mg; Total Carbohydrate 32g (Dietary Fiber 0g) **Exchanges:** ½ Starch, 1½ Other Carbohydrate, 3½ Fat **Carbohydrate Choices:** 2

 Pie Tip Serve these elegant tarts the next time you are entertaining because they can be made up to a day ahead of time. Top with garnishes just before serving, and for an added touch, top each with a few fresh raspberries.

lemon mini tarts

Prep Time: 15 Minutes ✳ Start to Finish: 25 Minutes ✳ 16 mini tarts

FILLING

1 cup milk

1 box (4-serving size) lemon
 instant pudding and pie
 filling mix

1 teaspoon grated lemon peel

CRUST

1 Pillsbury refrigerated pie
 crust (from 15-oz box),
 softened as directed on box

GARNISH

Strawberry halves, lemon
 slices or other fresh fruit

Fresh mint leaves

Powdered sugar, if desired

1 Heat oven to 450°F. In medium bowl, beat milk and pudding mix with electric mixer on medium speed or with whisk 2 to 3 minutes until well blended. Stir in lemon peel. Cover and refrigerate.

2 Unroll pie crust on work surface. Using rolling pin, roll crust to 15-inch diameter. With lightly floured 3-inch round cutter, cut 16 rounds from crust; discard scraps. Fit rounds into 16 regular-size ungreased muffin cups, pressing in gently (see photo). Generously prick crusts with fork. Bake 5 to 7 minutes or until very light golden brown. Remove from pan; cool completely on cooling rack, about 15 minutes.

3 Spoon lemon filling into tart shells. Garnish with sliced fruit and mint leaves. Sprinkle with powdered sugar.

High Altitude (3500–6500 ft): No change.

1 Mini Tart: Calories 90; Total Fat 3.5g (Saturated Fat 1.5g; Trans Fat 0g); Cholesterol 0mg; Sodium 140mg; Total Carbohydrate 14g (Dietary Fiber 0g) **Exchanges:** 1 Other Carbohydrate, ½ Fat **Carbohydrate Choices:** 1

banana mini tarts: Substitute banana instant pudding mix for the lemon and omit the grated lemon peel. Garnish with sliced bananas and mint leaves.

Pie Tip To save time, bake and freeze the mini tarts up to 3 months ahead. Thaw at room temperature. Make the filling about 30 minutes before serving; cover and refrigerate. Fill the tart shells and garnish as desired.

Making Mini Tart Shells

Fit rounds into muffin cups, and gently press on bottoms and up sides.

key lime pecan tart

Sue Tyner | Tustin, CA | Bake-Off® Contest 42, 2006

Prep Time: 25 Minutes ✳ Start to Finish: 2 Hours 35 Minutes ✳ 12 servings

CRUST

1 Pillsbury refrigerated pie crust (from 15-oz box), softened as directed on box

FILLING

¼ cup Key lime or regular lime juice

½ envelope (1½ teaspoons) unflavored gelatin

1 package (8 oz) cream cheese, softened

1 box (4-serving size) lemon instant pudding and pie filling mix

3 containers (6 oz each) Key lime pie low-fat yogurt

½ cup sugar

½ cup chopped pecans

1 Heat oven to 450°F. Place pie crust in 10-inch tart pan with removable bottom as directed on box for One-Crust Filled Pie. Bake 9 to 11 minutes or until lightly browned. Cool completely on cooling rack, about 15 minutes.

2 Meanwhile, in 1-cup microwavable measuring cup or small bowl, place lime juice. Stir in gelatin. Microwave on High about 30 seconds, stirring occasionally, until gelatin is dissolved; set aside.

3 In large bowl, beat cream cheese with electric mixer on medium speed until light and fluffy. Add gelatin mixture and pudding mix; beat until smooth, scraping bowl frequently. Add 1 container of yogurt at a time, beating well after each addition. Gradually beat in sugar until smooth.

4 Spread filling evenly in cooled baked crust; sprinkle with pecans. Refrigerate at least 2 hours until chilled. To remove tart from sides of pan, place the pan on a wide, short can and pull down the side of the pan (see page 80). If necessary, use a thin-bladed knife to loosen crust from the side of the pan. Cover and refrigerate any remaining pie.

High Altitude (3500–6500 ft): No change.

1 Serving: Calories 320; Total Fat 15g (Saturated Fat 5g; Trans Fat 0g); Cholesterol 15mg; Sodium 320mg; Total Carbohydrate 42g (Dietary Fiber 0g) **Exchanges:** ½ Starch, 2 Other Carbohydrate, ½ Low-Fat Milk, 2 Fat **Carbohydrate Choices:** 3

Pie Tip Sprinkle the filling with flaked coconut rather than the chopped pecans for a nice flavor change.

fluffy key lime pie

Prep Time: 30 Minutes ✳ Start to Finish: 3 Hours 15 Minutes ✳ 8 servings

CRUST
1 Pillsbury refrigerated pie crust (from 15-oz box), softened as directed on box

FILLING
1 envelope unflavored gelatin

1 cup sugar

½ cup fresh Key lime or regular lime juice

¼ cup water

4 pasteurized eggs, separated*

1 teaspoon grated lime peel

2 drops green food color

1 cup whipping cream

TOPPING, IF DESIRED
Sweetened whipped cream

Lime wedges

1 Heat oven to 450°F. Bake pie crust as directed on box for One-Crust Baked Shell, using 9-inch glass pie plate. Cool completely on cooling rack, about 15 minutes.

2 Meanwhile, in 1-quart saucepan, mix gelatin, ½ cup of the sugar, the lime juice, water and egg yolks. Cook over medium heat 6 to 7 minutes, stirring constantly, until mixture boils and thickens slightly. Remove from heat; stir in lime peel and food color. Pour mixture into large bowl. Refrigerate until mixture mounds slightly, about 45 minutes.

3 In large bowl, beat egg whites with electric mixer on high speed until soft peaks form. Gradually add remaining ½ cup sugar, beating until stiff peaks form. In chilled small bowl, beat whipping cream until stiff peaks form.

4 Fold egg whites and whipped cream into cooled lime mixture. Spoon into cooled baked crust. Refrigerate until firm, about 2 hours. Serve topped with sweetened whipped cream. Garnish with lime wedges. Cover and refrigerate any remaining pie.

*Pasteurized eggs are uncooked eggs that have been heat-treated to kill bacteria. Because the egg whites in this recipe are not cooked, be sure to use pasteurized eggs. They can be found in the dairy case at large supermarkets.

High Altitude (3500–6500 ft): No change.

1 Serving: Calories 460; Total Fat 26g (Saturated Fat 12g; Trans Fat 0g); Cholesterol 145mg; Sodium 270mg; Total Carbohydrate 53g (Dietary Fiber 0g) **Exchanges:** 1½ Starch, 2 Other Carbohydrate, 5 Fat **Carbohydrate Choices:** 3½

Pie Tip The Key lime juice will give this pie a true Key lime flavor. Key limes are smaller in size than regular limes and have a distinct aroma. Key lime juice is also available in bottles.

orange mousse pie

Prep Time: 30 Minutes ✳ Start to Finish: 2 Hours 45 Minutes ✳ 8 servings

CRUST

1 Pillsbury refrigerated pie crust (from 15-oz box), softened as directed on box or Chocolate Cookie Crumb Crust (page 7)

FILLING

1 envelope unflavored gelatin

¾ cup orange juice

1 package (8 oz) cream cheese, softened

1 cup powdered sugar

1 teaspoon grated orange peel

2 cups whipping cream

2 large oranges, peeled, chopped and drained (2 cups)

TOPPING

Additional orange peel, if desired

1 container (6 oz) French vanilla low-fat yogurt

1 Heat oven to 450°F. Bake pie crust as directed on box for One-Crust Baked Shell, using 9-inch glass pie plate. Cool completely on cooling rack, about 15 minutes.

2 Meanwhile, in 1-quart saucepan, mix gelatin and orange juice; let stand 1 minute to soften. Cook and stir over medium heat until dissolved. In small bowl, beat cream cheese, powdered sugar and 1 teaspoon orange peel with electric mixer on medium speed until smooth and fluffy. Gradually add softened gelatin; blend well. Refrigerate until slightly thickened, about 15 minutes.

3 In chilled large bowl, beat whipping cream with electric mixer on high speed until stiff peaks form. Fold whipped cream into orange mixture; gently fold in chopped oranges. Spoon into cooled baked crust. Refrigerate until firm, about 2 hours. Garnish with orange peel. Top each serving with dollop of yogurt. Cover and refrigerate any remaining pie.

High Altitude (3500–6500 ft): No change.

1 Serving: Calories 520; Total Fat 36g (Saturated Fat 20g; Trans Fat 1g); Cholesterol 100mg; Sodium 230mg; Total Carbohydrate 45g (Dietary Fiber 1g) **Exchanges:** ½ Fruit, 2½ Other Carbohydrate, 1 High-Fat Meat, 5½ Fat **Carbohydrate Choices:** 3

 Pie Tip If you like mandarin oranges, you can substitute one 11-oz can, drained and coarsely chopped, for the 2 large oranges.

orange cheesecake pie

Prep Time: 30 Minutes ∗ Start to Finish: 1 Hour 40 Minutes ∗ 8 servings

CRUST

1 Pillsbury refrigerated pie crust (from 15-oz box), softened as directed on box

1 teaspoon sugar

FILLING

12 oz ⅓-less-fat cream cheese (Neufchâtel), softened

2 containers (6 oz each) orange crème low-fat yogurt

¼ cup powdered sugar

1 can (6 oz) frozen orange juice concentrate, thawed

1 box (4-serving size) cheesecake-flavor instant pudding and pie filling mix

1 container (8 oz) frozen light whipped topping, thawed

1 Heat oven to 450°F. Unroll crust on work surface. Sprinkle with sugar. With rolling pin, roll sugar into crust. Place crust, sugar side up, in 9-inch glass pie plate. Fold edges under; flute. Prick bottom and sides generously with fork. Bake 9 to 11 minutes or until lightly browned. Cool completely on cooling rack, about 20 minutes.

2 In large bowl, beat cream cheese, yogurt and powdered sugar with electric mixer on high speed until light and fluffy. Add orange juice concentrate; beat on medium speed until well blended. Sprinkle pie filling mix over top; beat on low speed until well mixed.

3 Reserve 1 cup of the whipped topping for garnish. Fold remaining whipped topping into cream cheese mixture until well blended.

4 Spread filling evenly in cooled baked crust. Refrigerate at least 1 hour or until set. Garnish with reserved whipped topping, and if desired, grated orange peel. Refrigerate any remaining pie.

High Altitude (3500–6500 ft): No change.

1 Serving: Calories 560; Total Fat 29g (Saturated Fat 15g; Trans Fat 0g); Cholesterol 45mg; Sodium 630mg; Total Carbohydrate 66g (Dietary Fiber 0g) **Exchanges:** 2 Starch, ½ Fruit, 1½ Other Carbohydrate, ½ Low-Fat Milk, 5 Fat **Carbohydrate Choices:** 4½

Pie Tip For extra color and flavor, sprinkle each serving with grated chocolate or garnish with chocolate curls.

black-bottom peanut butter pie

Claudia Shepardson | South Yarmouth, MA | Bake-Off® Contest 42, 2006

Prep Time: 25 Minutes ✳ Start to Finish: 3 Hours 25 Minutes ✳ 8 servings

CRUST
1 Pillsbury refrigerated pie crust (from 15-oz box), softened as directed on box

FUDGE LAYER
1¼ cups dark or semisweet chocolate chips

½ cup whipping cream

2 tablespoons butter or margarine, melted

FILLING
1¼ cups milk

1 container (6 oz) French vanilla fat-free yogurt

1 box (4-serving size) white chocolate instant pudding and pie filling mix

3 tablespoons butter or margarine

1 bag (10 oz) peanut butter chips (1⅔ cups)

TOPPING
4 peanut butter crunchy granola bars (2 pouches from 8.9-oz box), crushed (¾ cup)

1 Heat oven to 450°F. Make pie crust as directed on box for One-Crust Baked Shell, using 9-inch glass pie plate. Cool completely on cooling rack, about 15 minutes.

2 Meanwhile, in 1-quart heavy saucepan, mix fudge layer ingredients. Cook over low heat, stirring constantly, until chips are melted. Remove from heat; stir until smooth. Reserve ¼ cup fudge mixture in small microwavable bowl for drizzle; set remaining mixture aside to cool.

3 In large bowl, beat milk, yogurt and pudding mix with electric mixer on high speed about 3 minutes or until smooth and thickened. Set aside.

4 In another small microwavable bowl, microwave 3 tablespoons butter and the peanut butter chips uncovered on High 45 seconds. Stir; if necessary, continue to microwave in 10-second increments, stirring after each, until chips are melted and mixture is smooth. On low speed, gradually beat peanut butter mixture into pudding mixture until combined; beat on high speed until filling is smooth and fluffy, scraping side of bowl occasionally.

5 Spread cooled fudge layer mixture evenly into cooled baked crust. Carefully spoon and spread filling evenly over fudge layer. Sprinkle crushed granola bars evenly over top. Refrigerate until set, 3 to 4 hours .

6 To serve, microwave reserved ¼ cup fudge mixture uncovered on High 15 to 20 seconds or until drizzling consistency. Drizzle over top of pie. Cover and refrigerate any remaining pie.

High Altitude (3500–6500 ft): No change.

1 Serving: Calories 690; Total Fat 40g (Saturated Fat 18g; Trans Fat 0g); Cholesterol 45mg; Sodium 520mg; Total Carbohydrate 72g (Dietary Fiber 4g) **Exchanges:** 1 Starch, 4 Other Carbohydrate, 1 High-Fat Meat, 6 Fat **Carbohydrate Choices:** 5

Pie Tip To easily crush the granola bars, don't unwrap them. Use a rolling pin and crush the bars in the wrappers—makes cleanup a snap!

candy bar pie

Tracey Chrenko | Owosso, MI | Bake-Off® Contest 35, 1992

Prep Time: 20 Minutes ✳ Start to Finish: 5 Hours ✳ 10 servings

CRUST

1 Pillsbury refrigerated pie
  crust (from 15-oz box),
  softened as directed on box

FILLING

5 bars (2.07 oz each) milk
  chocolate–covered peanut,
  caramel and nougat candy

4 packages (3 oz each) cream
  cheese, softened

½ cup sugar

2 eggs

⅓ cup sour cream

⅓ cup creamy peanut butter

TOPPING

3 tablespoons whipping cream

⅔ cup milk chocolate chips

1 Heat oven to 450°F. Place pie crust in 9-inch glass pie plate as directed on box for One-Crust Filled Pie. Bake 5 to 7 minutes or until very light golden brown. Cool while preparing filling. Reduce oven temperature to 325°F.

2 Cut candy bars in half lengthwise; cut into ¼-inch pieces. Place candy bar pieces over bottom of partially baked crust. In small bowl, beat cream cheese and sugar with electric mixer on medium speed until smooth. Beat in 1 egg at a time until well blended. Add sour cream and peanut butter, beating until mixture is smooth. Pour over candy bar pieces. Bake at 325°F 30 to 40 minutes or until center is set. Cool completely on cooling rack, about 2 hours.

3 In 1-quart saucepan, heat whipping cream until very warm. Remove from heat; stir in chocolate chips until melted and smooth. Spread over top of pie. Refrigerate 2 to 3 hours or until set before serving. Garnish with candy pieces, if desired. Cover and refrigerate any remaining pie.

High Altitude (3500–6500 ft): In step 1, bake 6 to 8 minutes. In step 2, bake 35 to 45 minutes.

1 Serving: Calories 560; Total Fat 36g (Saturated Fat 18g; Trans Fat 0g); Cholesterol 95mg; Sodium 320mg; Total Carbohydrate 48g (Dietary Fiber 1g) **Exchanges:** 3 Other Carbohydrate, 1½ High-Fat Meat, 5 Fat **Carbohydrate Choices:** 3

pear and ginger cream tart

Prep Time: 45 Minutes ✴ Start to Finish: 1 Hour 45 Minutes ✴ 8 servings

PASTRY CREAM

1½ cups milk

1 tablespoon grated gingerroot

4 egg yolks

¾ cup sugar

½ cup all-purpose flour

2 tablespoons butter or
  margarine

1½ teaspoons vanilla

CRUST

1 Pillsbury refrigerated pie
  crust (from 15-oz box),
  softened as directed on box

TOPPING

2 cans (15 oz each) pear halves
  in juice, drained

1 oz white chocolate baking
  bar (from 6-oz package)

1 teaspoon shortening

1 In 3-quart saucepan, heat milk and grated gingerroot over low heat about 5 minutes, stirring frequently, until very hot but not boiling.

2 In medium bowl, beat egg yolks and sugar with electric mixer on medium speed 4 to 6 minutes or until pale yellow. Beat in flour. Gradually beat in warm milk mixture until well blended.

3 Return mixture to saucepan; cook over medium-low heat about 5 minutes, stirring constantly, until mixture is very thick and begins to boil. Boil 1 minute, stirring constantly. Remove from heat; stir in butter and vanilla. Pour into medium bowl; place plastic wrap on surface of pastry cream. Refrigerate until completely cooled, about 1 hour.

4 Meanwhile, heat oven to 450°F. Bake pie crust as directed on box for One-Crust Baked Shell, using 9-inch tart pan with removable bottom or 9-inch glass pie plate. Trim edges if necessary. Cool completely on cooling rack, about 15 minutes.

5 Fill cooled baked crust with pastry cream. Cut pear halves into thin slices; arrange over pastry cream.

6 In small microwavable bowl, microwave baking bar and shortening uncovered on High 45 to 60 seconds, stirring once halfway through microwaving, until melted. If necessary, continue to microwave on High in 15-second increments, stirring until smooth. Drizzle over tart. To remove tart from sides of pan, place the pan on a wide, short can and pull down the side of the pan (see page 80). If necessary, use a thin-bladed knife to loosen crust from the side of the pan. Cover and refrigerate any remaining tart.

High Altitude (3500–6500 ft): No change.

1 Serving: Calories 460; Total Fat 22g (Saturated Fat 9g; Trans Fat 0g); Cholesterol 120mg; Sodium 270mg; Total Carbohydrate 60g (Dietary Fiber 2g) **Exchanges:** 1 Starch, 3 Other Carbohydrate, 4½ Fat **Carbohydrate Choices:** 4

 Pie Tip Any leftover fresh gingerroot is easy to store in the freezer. Tightly wrap it and freeze up to 6 months. Grate what you need from the frozen gingerroot, rewrap and return it to the freezer.

tropical pineapple–cream cheese tart

Prep Time: 25 Minutes ✳ Start to Finish: 1 Hour 50 Minutes ✳ 10 servings

CRUST

1 Pillsbury refrigerated pie
crust (from 15-oz box),
softened as directed on box

1 teaspoon sugar

FILLING

1 package (8 oz) cream cheese,
softened

¼ cup sugar

1 teaspoon coconut extract

1 egg

TOPPING

1 can (20 oz) crushed
pineapple in syrup, well
drained, ¼ cup liquid
reserved

2 teaspoons cornstarch

1 Heat oven to 450°F. Unroll pie crust on work surface. Sprinkle with
1 teaspoon sugar; roll in lightly with rolling pin. Press crust, sugar side up,
in bottom and up side of 10- or 9-inch tart pan with removable bottom.
Trim edges if necessary.

2 Bake 7 to 9 minutes or until light golden brown. Cool partially baked crust
on cooling rack while preparing filling. Reduce oven temperature to 400°F.

3 In small bowl, beat cream cheese with electric mixer on medium speed
until light and fluffy. Add ¼ cup sugar, the coconut extract and egg;
beat until well blended. Pour into partially baked crust. Carefully spoon
pineapple over cream cheese mixture. (Pineapple will not completely
cover cream cheese.)

4 Bake at 400°F 20 to 25 minutes or until filling is puffed around edges
and set.

5 Meanwhile, in 1-quart saucepan, mix reserved ¼ cup pineapple liquid and
the cornstarch until smooth. Cook over medium heat, stirring frequently,
until glaze boils and thickens.

6 Spoon pineapple glaze over pineapple. Cool completely, about 1 hour,
before serving. To remove tart from sides of pan, place the pan on a wide,
short can and pull down the side of the pan (see page 80). If necessary, use
a thin-bladed knife to loosen crust from the side of the pan. Cover and
refrigerate any remaining pie.

High Altitude (3500–6500 ft): For pineapple topping, reserve ⅓ cup pineapple
liquid. In step 4, bake 25 to 30 minutes.

1 Serving: Calories 340; Total Fat 20g (Saturated Fat 9g; Trans Fat 0g); Cholesterol 50mg; Sodium
250mg; Total Carbohydrate 37g (Dietary Fiber 0g) **Exchanges:** 1 Starch, 1½ Other Carbohydrate, 3½ Fat
Carbohydrate Choices: 2½

 Pie Tip Because many people like the flavor of coconut but not its
texture, coconut extract was added to the filling. If you like
coconut, sprinkle toasted coconut over the filling before adding the pineapple glaze.

raspberry mousse pie

Prep Time: 25 Minutes ✻ Start to Finish: 3 Hours 30 Minutes ✻ 8 servings

CRUST

1 Pillsbury refrigerated pie crust (from 15-oz box), softened as directed on box

½ cup almond paste (from 8-oz tube)

FILLING

2 cups whipping cream

1 envelope unflavored gelatin

2 tablespoons cold water

1 tablespoon lemon juice

4 cups fresh or frozen raspberries (from two 12-oz bags)

¾ cup sugar

SAUCE

3 tablespoons sugar

3 tablespoons frozen cranberry-raspberry juice concentrate, thawed

GARNISH

Mint sprigs, if desired

1 Heat oven to 450°F. Bake pie crust as directed on box for One-Crust Baked Shell, using 9-inch glass pie plate.

2 Meanwhile, in small microwavable bowl, place almond paste and 2 tablespoons of the whipping cream. Microwave uncovered on High about 30 seconds or until almond paste is softened; stir until smooth. Spread almond paste mixture evenly over bottom of warm pie crust. Cool completely on cooling rack, about 45 minutes.

3 In small bowl, mix gelatin with cold water and lemon juice; stir with fork to soften. In 2-quart saucepan, mix 3 cups of the raspberries and ¾ cup sugar; add softened gelatin. Cook over medium heat 6 to 8 minutes, stirring constantly, until gelatin is dissolved and mixture is warm. Refrigerate until cool, about 30 minutes.

4 In chilled large bowl, beat remaining whipping cream with electric mixer on high speed until soft peaks form. Gently fold raspberry mixture into whipped cream. Spoon mixture over almond paste mixture. Refrigerate at least 2 hours or until chilled.

5 In medium bowl, place remaining 1 cup raspberries, 3 tablespoons sugar and the juice concentrate. Crush raspberries with fork and stir well to dissolve sugar. Drizzle crushed raspberry mixture over individual servings of pie. Garnish with fresh mint. Cover and refrigerate any remaining pie.

High Altitude (3500–6500 ft): No change.

1 Serving: Calories 510; Total Fat 29g (Saturated Fat 14g; Trans Fat 0.5g); Cholesterol 70mg; Sodium 135mg; Total Carbohydrate 57g (Dietary Fiber 5g) **Exchanges:** 1 Starch, ½ Fruit, 2½ Other Carbohydrate, 5½ Fat **Carbohydrate Choices:** 4

strawberry mousse pie: Substitute 4 cups small fresh or unsweetened frozen strawberries for the raspberries.

 Pie Tip Be sure the pie crust is warm when spreading the almond paste mixture over the crust. The warm crust will help keep the almond paste mixture soft and easier to spread.

raspberry-lemon meringue tart

Prep Time: 1 Hour ✳ Start to Finish: 4 Hours ✳ 8 servings

RASPBERRY FILLING

1 bag (12 oz) frozen whole raspberries

¼ cup sugar

2 tablespoons cornstarch

CRUST

1 Pillsbury refrigerated pie crust (from 15-oz box), softened as directed on box

LEMON FILLING

1 cup sugar

2 tablespoons cornstarch

2 tablespoons all-purpose flour

¼ teaspoon salt

1½ cups water

3 egg yolks, beaten

1 tablespoon grated lemon peel

⅓ cup lemon juice

1 tablespoon butter or margarine

MERINGUE

⅓ cup sugar

1 tablespoon cornstarch

⅓ cup water

3 egg whites

⅛ teaspoon salt

1 Place raspberries on large platter to thaw, about 1 hour. When thawed, place in strainer over bowl to collect juices.

2 Heat oven to 450°F. Bake pie crust as directed on box for One-Crust Baked Shell, using 9-inch tart pan with removable bottom or 9-inch glass pie plate. Cool completely on cooling rack, about 15 minutes.

3 In 2-quart saucepan, mix ¼ cup sugar and 2 tablespoons cornstarch. If necessary, add water to reserved raspberry liquid to measure ½ cup; gradually add raspberry liquid to sugar mixture. Cook over medium heat, stirring constantly, until thickened. Gently fold in raspberries. Cool 10 minutes. Spread evenly in cooled baked crust.

4 In 2-quart saucepan, mix 1 cup sugar, 2 tablespoons cornstarch, the flour and ¼ teaspoon salt. Gradually stir in 1½ cups water, stirring until smooth. Heat to boiling over medium heat; cook and stir 1 minute longer. Remove from heat. Quickly stir about ½ cup hot mixture into beaten egg yolks; mix well. Gradually stir egg mixture back into hot mixture. Stir in lemon peel and juice. Cook over medium heat about 5 minutes, stirring constantly. Remove from heat. Add butter; stir until melted. Let stand 10 minutes.

5 Meanwhile, heat oven to 350°F. In 1-quart saucepan, mix ⅓ cup sugar and 1 tablespoon cornstarch. Stir in ⅓ cup water; cook and stir over medium heat until thickened. Cool completely by placing in freezer about 15 minutes. In small bowl, beat egg whites and ⅛ teaspoon salt with electric mixer on high speed until soft peaks form. Add cooled cornstarch mixture, beating on medium speed until stiff peaks form. Carefully pour hot lemon filling over raspberry mixture in crust. Gently spread meringue over filling. Bake 20 to 25 minutes or until meringue reaches 160°F. Cool 2 hours; refrigerate until serving time. To remove tart from sides of pan, place the pan on a wide, short can and pull down the side of the pan (see page 80).

High Altitude (over 3500 ft): Not recommended.

1 Serving: Calories 370; Total Fat 10g (Saturated Fat 4g; Trans Fat 0g); Cholesterol 85mg; Sodium 260mg; Total Carbohydrate 65g (Dietary Fiber 3g) **Exchanges:** 1 Starch, 3½ Other Carbohydrate, 2 Fat **Carbohydrate Choices:** 4

plum–cream cheese tart

Prep Time: 15 Minutes ✳ Start to Finish: 2 Hours ✳ 8 servings

CRUST

1 Pillsbury refrigerated pie
crust (from 15-oz box),
softened as directed on box

FILLING

2 packages (3 oz each) cream
cheese, softened

¾ cup powdered sugar

1 teaspoon grated orange peel

2 eggs

2 large plums, pitted, sliced

2 tablespoons red currant jelly,
melted

1 Heat oven to 450°F. Place pie crust in 9-inch tart pan with removable bottom or 9-inch glass pie plate. Trim edges if necessary. Generously prick crust with fork. Bake about 7 minutes or until very lightly brown. Cool on cooling rack 5 minutes. Reduce oven temperature to 325°F.

2 Meanwhile, in small bowl, beat cream cheese and powdered sugar with electric mixer on low speed until smooth. Add orange peel and eggs; beat until smooth and well blended. Spread in partially baked crust. Arrange sliced plums over cream cheese filling.

3 Bake at 325°F 25 to 30 minutes or until filling is set. Cool on cooling rack 15 minutes. Refrigerate at least 1 hour or until chilled. Just before serving, brush melted jelly over tart. To remove tart from sides of pan, place the pan on a wide, short can and pull down the side of the pan (see page 80). If necessary, use a thin-bladed knife to loosen crust from the side of the pan. Cover and refrigerate any remaining tart.

High Altitude (3500–6500 ft): In step 3, bake 30 to 35 minutes.

1 Serving: Calories 400; Total Fat 23g (Saturated Fat 10g; Trans Fat 0g); Cholesterol 80mg; Sodium 300mg; Total Carbohydrate 44g (Dietary Fiber 0g) **Exchanges:** 1 Starch, 1 Fruit, 1 Other Carbohydrate, 4½ Fat **Carbohydrate Choices:** 3

Pie Tip For the sweetest flavor, choose ripe plums. To speed up the ripening process, seal the plums in a brown paper bag for a day or two. The size of plums varies; if they are small, buy one or two additional plums.

strawberries and cream tart

Prep Time: 40 Minutes ✳ Start to Finish: 1 Hour 10 Minutes ✳ 10 servings

CRUST

1 Pillsbury refrigerated pie
crust (from 15-oz box),
softened as directed on box

FILLING

1 package (8 oz) cream cheese,
softened

⅓ cup sugar

¼ to ½ teaspoon almond
extract

1 cup whipping cream,
whipped

TOPPING

4 cups fresh strawberries,
washed, hulled and halved

½ cup semisweet chocolate
chips

1 tablespoon shortening

1 Heat oven to 450°F. Bake pie crust as directed on box for One-Crust Baked Shell, using 10-inch tart pan or 9-inch glass pie plate. Cool completely on cooling rack, about 15 minutes.

2 In large bowl, beat cream cheese with electric mixer on medium speed until fluffy. Gradually add sugar and almond extract; beat well. Fold in whipped cream. Spoon filling into cooled baked crust.

3 Arrange strawberry halves over filling. Refrigerate while making topping. In 1-quart saucepan, melt chocolate chips and shortening over low heat, stirring constantly, until smooth. Drizzle over strawberries and filling. Refrigerate until set, about 30 minutes. To remove tart from sides of pan, place the pan on a wide, short can and pull down the side of the pan (see page 80). If necessary, use a thin-bladed knife to loosen crust from the side of the pan. Cover and refrigerate any remaining tart.

High Altitude (3500–6500 ft): No change.

1 Serving: Calories 350; Total Fat 25g (Saturated Fat 13g; Trans Fat 0.5g); Cholesterol 55mg; Sodium 160mg; Total Carbohydrate 28g (Dietary Fiber 1g) **Exchanges:** 2 Other Carbohydrate, ½ High-Fat Meat, 4 Fat **Carbohydrate Choices:** 2

 For a different look, use small whole strawberries, and dip the pointed end of each strawberry into melted chocolate so it's half covered. Set stem-end-down on a waxed paper–lined tray. Chill until set. Arrange on top of chilled filling.

chocolate, coffee and oatmeal pie

Prep Time: 45 Minutes ✳ Start to Finish: 4 Hours 40 Minutes ✳ 8 servings

CRUST

1 Pillsbury refrigerated pie crust (from 15-oz box), softened as directed on box

FILLING

3 eggs

¾ cup sugar

¾ cup dark corn syrup

3 tablespoons coffee-flavored liqueur or cold strong coffee

2 tablespoons butter or margarine, melted, cooled

¼ teaspoon salt

½ cup quick-cooking oats

1 cup semisweet chocolate chips (6 oz)

1 Heat oven to 450°F. Unroll crust on work surface. Sprinkle both sides of crust with flour. Place crust in 9-inch glass pie plate as directed on box for One-Crust Filled Pie—except do not prick crust. Bake 9 to 11 minutes or until lightly browned. If crust has risen in center, press down gently with back of spoon. Cool completely on cooling rack, about 15 minutes. Reduce oven temperature to 350°F.

2 Meanwhile, in medium bowl, whisk eggs until blended. Add sugar, corn syrup, liqueur, butter and salt; mix well. Stir in oats and chocolate chips. Pour filling into crust-lined pie plate. Cover crust edge with foil to prevent excessive browning.

3 Bake at 350°F 45 to 55 minutes or until top is golden brown and center is almost set. Cool at least 3 hours before serving. Cover and refrigerate any remaining pie.

High Altitude (3500–6500 ft): No change.

1 Serving: Calories 480; Total Fat 19g (Saturated Fat 9g; Trans Fat 0g); Cholesterol 90mg; Sodium 270mg; Total Carbohydrate 74g (Dietary Fiber 2g) **Exchanges:** 1 Starch, 4 Other Carbohydrate, 3½ Fat **Carbohydrate Choices:** 5

Pie Tip This pie is a close cousin to pecan pie. Instead of pecans, the oatmeal rises to the surface of the pie during baking and forms the chewy top layer. Serve with a generous spoonful of whipped cream.

oats 'n honey granola pie

Suzanne Conrad | Findlay, OH | Bake-Off® Contest 41, 2004

Prep Time: 15 Minutes ✳ Start to Finish: 1 Hour 35 Minutes ✳ 8 servings

CRUST
1 Pillsbury refrigerated pie
  crust (from 15-oz box),
  softened as directed on box

FILLING
½ cup butter or margarine

½ cup packed light brown
  sugar

¾ cup corn syrup

⅛ teaspoon salt

1 teaspoon vanilla

3 eggs, slightly beaten

4 oats 'n honey crunchy
  granola bars (2 pouches
  from 8.9-oz box), crushed
  (¾ cup)

½ cup chopped walnuts

¼ cup quick-cooking or
  old-fashioned oats

¼ cup chocolate chips

SERVE WITH, IF DESIRED
Whipped cream or ice cream

1 Heat oven to 350°F. Unroll crust on work surface. Sprinkle both sides of crust with flour. Place crust in 9-inch glass pie plate as directed on box for One-Crust Filled Pie.

2 In large microwavable bowl, microwave butter uncovered on High 50 to 60 seconds or until melted. Stir in brown sugar and corn syrup until blended. Beat in salt, vanilla and eggs until blended. Stir in remaining filling ingredients. Pour filling into crust-lined pie plate. Cover crust edge with foil to prevent excessive browning; remove foil during last 15 minutes of bake time.

3 Bake 40 to 50 minutes or until filling is set and crust is golden brown. Cool at least 30 minutes before serving. Serve warm, at room temperature or chilled with whipped cream. Cover and refrigerate any remaining pie.

High Altitude (3500–6500 ft): No change.

1 Serving: Calories 540; Total Fat 29g (Saturated Fat 12g; Trans Fat 0g); Cholesterol 115mg; Sodium 320mg; Total Carbohydrate 64g (Dietary Fiber 1g) **Exchanges:** 1½ Starch, 3 Other Carbohydrate, 5 Fat **Carbohydrate Choices:** 4

Pie Tip | To easily crush the granola bars, don't unwrap them. Use a rolling pin and crush the bars in the wrappers—this makes cleanup a snap!

chocolate surprise pecan pie

Prep Time: 25 Minutes ✳ Start to Finish: 3 Hours 10 Minutes ✳ 10 servings

CRUST

1 Pillsbury refrigerated pie crust (from 15-oz box), softened as directed on box

FILLING

1 package (8 oz) cream cheese, softened

⅓ cup sugar

Dash salt

1 teaspoon vanilla

1 egg

1 cup chopped pecans

½ cup semisweet chocolate chips

TOPPING

3 eggs

¼ cup sugar

1 cup light corn syrup

1 teaspoon vanilla

1 oz unsweetened baking chocolate, melted, cooled

GARNISH

½ cup whipping cream

1 tablespoon chocolate-flavor syrup

1 Heat oven to 375°F. Unroll crust on work surface. Sprinkle both sides of crust with flour. Place crust in 9-inch glass pie plate as directed on box for One-Crust Filled Pie. In small bowl, beat cream cheese, ⅓ cup sugar, the salt, 1 teaspoon vanilla and 1 egg with electric mixer on low speed until well blended. Spread cream cheese mixture evenly in bottom of crust-lined pie plate. Sprinkle with pecans and chocolate chips.

2 In small bowl, beat topping ingredients with electric mixer on medium speed just until blended. Carefully pour topping over pecans and chocolate chips. Cover crust edge with foil to prevent excessive browning; remove foil during last 15 minutes of bake time.

3 Bake 40 to 45 minutes or until center is set. Cool on cooling rack at least 2 hours before serving.

4 In chilled small bowl, beat whipping cream with electric mixer on high speed until stiff peaks form. To serve, drizzle each pie piece with chocolate syrup. Spoon dollop of whipped cream on top. Cover and refrigerate any remaining pie.

High Altitude (3500–6500 ft): In step 3, bake 60 to 65 minutes.

1 Serving: Calories 540; Total Fat 31g (Saturated Fat 13g; Trans Fat 0g); Cholesterol 125mg; Sodium 220mg; Total Carbohydrate 58g (Dietary Fiber 2g) **Exchanges:** ½ Starch, 3½ Other Carbohydrate, ½ High-Fat Meat, 5½ Fat **Carbohydrate Choices:** 4

 Pie Tip You can quickly soften the cream cheese in the microwave. Remove from wrapper, and place the cream cheese on a microwavable plate; microwave uncovered on High about 15 seconds or just until softened.

berry ice cream pie

Prep Time: 25 Minutes ✳ Start to Finish: 2 Hours 55 Minutes ✳ 8 servings

FILLING

3 cups (1½ pints) vanilla ice cream

2 cups (1 pint) raspberry sherbet

1 box (10 oz) frozen raspberries in syrup, thawed

CRUST

1 Pillsbury refrigerated pie crust (from 15-oz box), softened as directed on box

SAUCE

3 tablespoons sugar

1 tablespoon cornstarch

Reserved raspberry liquid

2 tablespoons orange juice

GARNISH

1 container (6 oz) fresh raspberries, if desired

1 Place ice cream and sherbet in refrigerator to soften. Place thawed raspberries and syrup in strainer over 2-cup glass measuring cup on counter to drain. Reserve liquid for sauce.

2 Heat oven to 450°F. Bake pie crust as directed on box for One-Crust Baked Shell, using 9-inch glass pie plate. Cool completely on cooling rack, about 15 minutes.

3 Scoop 1½ cups ice cream into cooled baked crust. In large bowl, fold drained raspberries into sherbet. Spoon mixture over ice cream. Scoop remaining ice cream over top. Freeze at least 2 hours until firm.

4 Meanwhile, in 1-quart saucepan, mix sugar and cornstarch. Stir in reserved raspberry liquid. Cook over medium heat, stirring constantly, until mixture becomes clear and thickened. Stir in orange juice. Cool at room temperature at least 10 minutes before serving. Serve individual pieces of pie with sauce. Garnish with fresh raspberries. Cover and freeze any remaining pie and sauce.

High Altitude (3500–6500 ft): No change.

1 Serving: Calories 450; Total Fat 20g (Saturated Fat 9g; Trans Fat 0g); Cholesterol 30mg; Sodium 280mg; Total Carbohydrate 64g (Dietary Fiber 2g) **Exchanges:** 1 Starch, 3 Other Carbohydrate, 4 Fat **Carbohydrate Choices:** 4

 For easier spreading, stir the ice cream smooth before spreading it on top of the pie. For a fun pie, instead of layering the sherbet and the ice cream, you can fold and swirl them together, and then spoon it into the pie crust.

buster sundae pie

Prep Time: 25 Minutes ✳ Start to Finish: 4 Hours 40 Minutes ✳ 8 servings

CRUST
1 Pillsbury refrigerated pie crust (from 15-oz box), softened as directed on box

FILLING AND TOPPING
1 quart (4 cups) vanilla ice cream, slightly softened

½ cup caramel topping

½ cup fudge topping

¾ cup Spanish peanuts (4 oz)

Additional peanuts, if desired

1 Heat oven to 450°F. Bake pie crust as directed on box for One-Crust Baked Shell, using 9-inch glass pie plate. Cool completely on cooling rack, about 15 minutes.

2 Spread 2 cups of the ice cream in cooled baked crust. Drizzle with ¼ cup caramel topping and ¼ cup fudge topping. Sprinkle with peanuts. Spread remaining 2 cups ice cream over peanuts. Freeze until firm, at least 4 hours or overnight.

3 Drizzle individual servings with remaining ¼ cup caramel topping and ¼ cup fudge topping. Sprinkle with peanuts. Cover and freeze any remaining pie.

High Altitude (3500–6500 ft): No change.

1 Serving: Calories 700; Total Fat 38g (Saturated Fat 16g; Trans Fat 0.5g); Cholesterol 70mg; Sodium 470mg; Total Carbohydrate 77g (Dietary Fiber 3g) **Exchanges:** 1½ Starch, 3½ Other Carbohydrate, 1 High-Fat Meat, 6 Fat **Carbohydrate Choices:** 5

Pie Tip For chocolate lovers, use 1 quart (4 cups) chocolate ice cream, slightly softened, instead of the vanilla ice cream.

strawberry daiquiri pie

Prep Time: 25 Minutes ✳ Start to Finish: 2 Hours 25 Minutes ✳ 8 servings

CRUST

1 Pillsbury refrigerated pie crust (from 15-oz box), softened as directed on box or Graham Cracker Crumb Crust (page 7)

FILLING

1 box (10 oz) frozen strawberries in syrup

1 can (6 oz) frozen limeade concentrate

3 tablespoons rum, if desired

1 quart (4 cups) vanilla ice cream, slightly softened

GARNISH

Sweetened whipped cream, if desired

Fresh strawberries, if desired

1 Heat oven to 450°F. Bake pie crust as directed on box for One-Crust Baked Shell, using 9-inch glass pie plate. Cool baked shell in freezer or refrigerator 10 to 15 minutes.

2 Meanwhile, in food processor bowl with metal blade, place strawberries, limeade concentrate and rum; cover and process until well blended.

3 Spoon ice cream into food processor; cover and process using quick on-and-off motions until blended. Spoon filling into cooled baked crust. Freeze until set, at least 2 hours. Garnish with whipped cream and fresh strawberries. Cover and freeze any remaining pie.

High Altitude (3500–6500 ft): No change.

1 Serving: Calories 460; Total Fat 21g (Saturated Fat 9g; Trans Fat 0g); Cholesterol 35mg; Sodium 270mg; Total Carbohydrate 64g (Dietary Fiber 1g) **Exchanges:** 1 Starch, ½ Fruit, 3 Other Carbohydrate, 3½ Fat **Carbohydrate Choices:** 4

Pie Tip The filling can be made in a blender if you don't have a food processor. Place the strawberries, limeade concentrate and rum in the blender; cover and process until well blended. Pour the strawberry mixture into a large bowl; add the ice cream. Mix until well blended.

chocolate-almond ice cream pie

Prep Time: 30 Minutes   ✳   Start to Finish: 5 Hours 30 Minutes   ✳   8 servings

CRUST

3 tablespoons butter or margarine, melted

¾ cup sliced almonds

⅓ cup sugar

1 Pillsbury refrigerated pie crust (from 15-oz box), softened as directed on box

FILLING

1 quart (4 cups) chocolate ice cream, slightly softened

1 Heat oven to 400°F. In small bowl, mix melted butter, almonds and sugar. Spoon ⅓ of mixture into shallow baking pan; spread evenly. Bake 5 to 7 minutes, stirring once, until toasted. Set aside to cool, stirring once.

2 Meanwhile, place pie crust in 9-inch glass pie plate as directed on box for One-Crust Filled Pie—except do not prick crust. Spoon remaining ⅔ of almond mixture into bottom and up side of crust; press against crust.

3 Bake crust 12 to 14 minutes or until golden brown. Cool completely on cooling rack, about 1 hour.

4 Spoon ice cream into cooled baked crust. Sprinkle cooled almond mixture over ice cream. Freeze uncovered until firm, about 4 hours. Let pie stand at room temperature 10 minutes before cutting. Cover and freeze any remaining pie.

High Altitude (3500–6500 ft): No change.

1 Serving: Calories 720; Total Fat 43g (Saturated Fat 18g; Trans Fat 1g); Cholesterol 50mg; Sodium 490mg; Total Carbohydrate 79g (Dietary Fiber 3g) **Exchanges:** 2½ Starch, 3 Other Carbohydrate, 8 Fat **Carbohydrate Choices:** 5

caramel-cashew ice cream pie: Substitute 1 quart (4 cups) caramel ice cream for the chocolate ice cream and ¾ cup coarsely chopped cashews for the almonds.

Pie Tip This is the perfect pie to have on hand for last-minute entertaining. It can be stored in the freezer up to 1 week.

coffee ice cream pie

Prep Time: 20 Minutes ✳ Start to Finish: 2 Hours 35 Minutes ✳ 8 servings

CRUST

1 Pillsbury refrigerated pie crust (from 15-oz box), softened as directed on box or Chocolate Cookie Crumb Crust (page 7)

¼ cup finely chopped cashews or macadamia nuts

FILLING

1 quart (4 cups) coffee ice cream, slightly softened

TOPPING

1 cup hot fudge topping, warmed

Whole cashews or macadamia nuts, if desired

1 Heat oven to 450°F. Make pie crust as directed on box for One-Crust Baked Shell, using 9-inch glass pie plate—except before baking, sprinkle chopped cashews over bottom of crust; lightly press into crust. Bake 10 to 12 minutes or until lightly browned. Cool completely on cooling rack, about 15 minutes.

2 Carefully spoon softened ice cream into cooled baked crust; smooth top with back of spoon. Cover and freeze about 2 hours or until firm.

3 To serve, remove pie from freezer and let stand 10 to 15 minutes. Top each serving with fudge topping; garnish with whole cashews. Cover and freeze any remaining pie.

High Altitude (3500–6500 ft): No change.

1 Serving: Calories 310; Total Fat 13g (Saturated Fat 7g; Trans Fat 0g); Cholesterol 30mg; Sodium 200mg; Total Carbohydrate 42g (Dietary Fiber 1g) **Exchanges:** 2½ Other Carbohydrate, ½ Low-Fat Milk, 2 Fat **Carbohydrate Choices:** 3

strawberry ice cream pie: Substitute 1 quart (4 cups) strawberry or vanilla ice cream, slightly softened, for the coffee ice cream and 1 cup strawberry ice cream topping for the hot fudge topping.

holiday pies and tarts

Three-Berry Cheesecake Pie, page 156

brown butter creamy apple pie

Lola Nebel | Cambridge, MN | Bake-Off® Contest 37, 1996

Prep Time: 45 Minutes ✳ Start to Finish: 3 Hours 15 Minutes ✳ 8 servings

CRUST

1 Pillsbury refrigerated pie crust (from 15-oz box), softened as directed on box

FILLING

¼ cup butter (do not use margarine)*

½ cup granulated sugar

1 egg

2 tablespoons all-purpose flour

1 teaspoon vanilla

3 large Granny Smith apples (about 2 lb), peeled, cut into ½-inch wedges

STREUSEL

½ cup all-purpose flour

¼ cup granulated sugar

¼ cup packed brown sugar

¾ teaspoon ground cinnamon

¼ cup cold butter or margarine

TOPPING

½ cup whipping cream

1 tablespoon powdered sugar

¼ teaspoon ground cinnamon

½ teaspoon vanilla

1 Heat oven to 400°F. Place pie crust in 9-inch glass pie plate as directed on box for One-Crust Filled Pie. In 1-quart saucepan, heat ¼ cup butter over medium heat, stirring constantly, until melted and lightly browned. Cool completely, about 15 minutes.

2 In small bowl, beat ½ cup granulated sugar and the egg with whisk until light and fluffy. Stir in 2 tablespoons flour and 1 teaspoon vanilla. With whisk, beat in cooled butter. Pour into crust-lined pie plate. Arrange apple wedges over top.

3 In medium bowl, mix all streusel ingredients except butter. Cut in butter, using pastry blender (or fork or pulling 2 table knives in opposite directions), until mixture looks like coarse crumbs. Sprinkle over apples; press lightly.

4 Bake 20 minutes. Reduce oven temperature to 350°F. Bake 40 to 50 minutes longer or until apples are tender and crust is golden brown. If necessary, cover crust edge with foil after 15 to 20 minutes of baking to prevent excessive browning. Cool on cooling rack 1 hour 30 minutes.

5 In chilled small bowl, beat whipping cream with electric mixer on high speed until soft peaks form. Add remaining topping ingredients; beat until stiff peaks form. Pipe or spoon onto pie. If desired, sprinkle with ground cinnamon. Refrigerate any remaining pie.

*We recommend using only butter because it browns and has a nice rich flavor.

High Altitude (3500–6500 ft): In step 4, increase second bake time to 50 to 55 minutes.

1 Serving: Calories 460; Total Fat 24g (Saturated Fat 13g; Trans Fat 0.5g); Cholesterol 75mg; Sodium 210mg; Total Carbohydrate 57g (Dietary Fiber 1g) **Exchanges:** ½ Starch, 3½ Other Carbohydrate, 4½ Fat **Carbohydrate Choices:** 4

caramel-toffee-apple pie

Prep Time: 55 Minutes ✳ Start to Finish: 3 Hours 30 Minutes ✳ 8 servings

FILLING

6 cups sliced peeled apples
(6 medium)

¾ cup granulated sugar

1 tablespoon plus 2 teaspoons
cornstarch

1 tablespoon butter or
margarine

¾ teaspoon ground cinnamon

½ teaspoon ground nutmeg

1 container (4 oz) snack-size
cinnamon applesauce

Juice of ½ medium lemon
(2 tablespoons)

½ cup toffee caramel dip

CRUST

1 box (15 oz) Pillsbury
refrigerated pie crusts,
softened as directed on box

½ cup chopped pecans

1 egg, beaten

1½ tablespoons half-and-half
or milk

2 tablespoons white decorator
sugar crystals, if desired

1 Heat oven to 400°F. Cover cookie sheet with foil; set aside. In 4-quart saucepan, cook all filling ingredients except toffee caramel dip over medium heat about 5 minutes, stirring occasionally, until butter melts and mixture develops "juice."

2 Unroll 1 pie crust on work surface; smooth crust with hands. Sprinkle ¼ cup of the pecans on crust to within 1½ inches from edge. Using rolling pin, press pecans into crust without them breaking through other side of crust. Run metal spatula under crust; place in 9-inch glass pie plate, pecan side up.

3 Spoon half of the filling mixture into crust. Spoon dip onto filling mixture, using 1 teaspoon to spoon the dip and another teaspoon to scrape the dip out of the spoon, and spread evenly over top. Spoon other half of filling mixture on top.

4 Unroll second crust on work surface; smooth crust with hands. Sprinkle remaining ¼ cup pecans on crust to within 1½ inches from edge. Using rolling pin, press pecans into crust without them breaking through other side of crust. Place crust over top of filling, pecan side up. Seal edge and flute.

5 In small bowl, stir together egg and half-and-half; lightly brush over entire crust, including fluted edge, brushing gently on areas that have pecans. Sprinkle evenly with sugar crystals. Cut 2 slits in top crust. Place pie on foil-covered cookie sheet.

6 Bake 20 minutes. Reduce oven temperature to 350°F. Bake 40 to 45 minutes longer or until juice begins to bubble through slits in crust and crust is golden brown. Cool on cooling rack 1 hour 30 minutes before serving.

High Altitude (3500–6500 ft): In step 6, after reducing temperature to 350°F, bake about 45 minutes.

1 Serving: Calories 500; Total Fat 22g (Saturated Fat 7g; Trans Fat 0g); Cholesterol 40mg; Sodium 310mg; Total Carbohydrate 75g (Dietary Fiber 2g) **Exchanges:** ½ Starch, ½ Fruit, 4 Other Carbohydrate, 4 Fat **Carbohydrate Choices:** 5

Pie Tip Try two different varieties of apples for an interesting texture and flavor. Use 4 sweet apples such as Gala or Golden Delicious, which become quite soft when baked, and 2 tart apples such as Granny Smith or Haralson, which become tender but retain their shape.

apple–dried cranberry streusel pie

Prep Time: 15 Minutes ✻ Start to Finish: 1 Hour 30 Minutes ✻ 8 servings

CRUST
1 Pillsbury refrigerated pie
   crust (from 15-oz box),
   softened as directed on box

FILLING
2 cans (21 oz each) apple pie
   filling

1 cup sweetened dried
   cranberries

½ teaspoon ground cinnamon

STREUSEL
⅓ cup all-purpose flour

¼ cup packed brown sugar

3 tablespoons cold butter or
   margarine

1 Heat oven to 450°F. Make pie crust as directed on box for One-Crust Baked Shell, using 9-inch glass pie plate—except do not prick crust. Bake 9 to 11 minutes or until lightly browned. Reduce oven temperature to 400°F.

2 Meanwhile, in medium bowl, mix filling ingredients. In small bowl, mix flour and brown sugar. Cut in butter, using pastry blender (or fork or pulling 2 table knives in opposite directions), until mixture looks like coarse crumbs.

3 Spoon filling mixture into warm baked crust. Sprinkle streusel mixture evenly over filling.

4 Bake at 400°F 35 to 45 minutes or until topping is golden brown and filling bubbles. If necessary, after 5 to 10 minutes of baking, cover crust edge with foil to prevent excessive browning. Cool on cooling rack at least 30 minutes before serving.

High Altitude (3500–6500 ft): After adding pie filling mixture and crumb mixture, cover crust edge with strips of foil to prevent excessive browning. In step 4, bake at 400°F 40 to 50 minutes.

1 Serving: Calories 430; Total Fat 12g (Saturated Fat 5g; Trans Fat 0g); Cholesterol 15mg; Sodium 150mg; Total Carbohydrate 79g (Dietary Fiber 3g) **Exchanges:** 5 Other Carbohydrate, 2½ Fat **Carbohydrate Choices:** 5

Pie Tip The flavors of apple and cherry complement each other, so try dried cherries instead of dried cranberries for a flavor change.

cranberry-cheesecake tart

James Sloboden | Puyallup, WA | Bake-Off® Contest 34, 1990

Prep Time: 30 Minutes * Start to Finish: 4 Hours 5 Minutes * 10 servings

CRUST

1 Pillsbury refrigerated pie crust (from 15-oz box), softened as directed on box

FILLING

1 can (16 oz) whole berry cranberry sauce

¼ cup chopped pecans

6 tablespoons sugar

1 tablespoon cornstarch

1 package (8 oz) cream cheese, softened

⅓ cup sugar

1 egg

TOPPING

1 cup sour cream

2 tablespoons sugar

½ teaspoon vanilla

1 Heat oven to 450°F. Bake pie crust as directed on box for One-Crust Baked Shell, using 10-inch tart pan with removable bottom or 9-inch glass pie plate. Cool on cooling rack 5 minutes. Reduce oven temperature to 375°F.

2 In medium bowl, mix cranberry sauce, pecans, 6 tablespoons sugar and the cornstarch. Spread in crust.

3 In medium bowl, beat cream cheese, ⅓ cup sugar and the egg with electric mixer on medium speed until smooth. Spoon evenly over cranberry mixture. Bake at 375°F 25 to 30 minutes or until set.

4 In small bowl, mix sour cream, 2 tablespoons sugar and the vanilla. Spoon evenly over filling. Bake at 375°F 5 minutes longer. Cool slightly. Refrigerate at least 3 hours or until set. To remove tart from sides of pan, place the pan on a wide, short can and pull down the side of the pan (see page 80). If necessary, use a thin-bladed knife to loosen crust from the side of the pan. Garnish with whole cranberries and fresh mint, if desired. Cover and refrigerate any remaining tart.

High Altitude (3500–6500 ft): No change.

1 Serving: Calories 390; Total Fat 20g (Saturated Fat 10g; Trans Fat 0g); Cholesterol 65mg; Sodium 180mg; Total Carbohydrate 47g (Dietary Fiber 0g) **Exchanges:** 1 Starch, 2 Other Carbohydrate, 4 Fat **Carbohydrate Choices:** 3

Pie Tip If you use a food processor to chop nuts, use short on-and-off motions to help prevent nuts from getting pasty.

apple, cranberry and fig tart

Prep Time: 30 Minutes ✱ Start to Finish: 1 Hour 35 Minutes ✱ 8 servings

CRUST

1 Pillsbury refrigerated pie crust (from 15-oz box), softened as directed on box

FILLING

¾ cup sugar

1 tablespoon cornstarch

¼ teaspoon ground nutmeg

4 cups thinly sliced, peeled apples (4 medium)

1 cup fresh or frozen cranberries

½ cup dried Calimyrna figs, stems removed, coarsely chopped

TOPPING

¼ cup sugar

¼ cup all-purpose flour

2 tablespoons butter or margarine, softened

Sweetened whipped cream

1 Heat oven to 450°F. Place pie crust in 10-inch tart pan with removable bottom or 9-inch glass pie plate. Trim edges; do not prick crust.

2 Bake 9 to 11 minutes or until golden brown. If necessary, with back of spoon, press any bubbles that may have formed during baking. Cool on cooling rack 5 minutes. Reduce oven temperature to 400°F.

3 In large bowl, mix ¾ cup sugar, the cornstarch and nutmeg. Gently stir in apples and cranberries until evenly coated. Sprinkle figs evenly in baked crust. Spoon apple mixture evenly over figs.

4 In small bowl, mix ¼ cup sugar and the flour. Cut in butter, using pastry blender (or fork or pulling 2 table knives through mixture in opposite directions), until mixture looks like coarse crumbs. Sprinkle over filling.

5 Bake at 400°F 40 to 50 minutes or until crust is deep golden brown and apples are tender. Lightly cover tart with foil after 30 minutes of bake time to prevent excessive browning. Cool on cooling rack at least 15 minutes before serving. To remove tart from sides of pan, place the pan on a wide, short can and pull down the side of the pan (see page 80). If necessary, use a thin-bladed knife to loosen crust from the side of the pan. Serve with whipped cream.

High Altitude (3500–6500 ft): Wrap pan with foil.

1 Serving: Calories 320; Total Fat 10g (Saturated Fat 4.5g; Trans Fat 0g); Cholesterol 10mg; Sodium 130mg; Total Carbohydrate 56g (Dietary Fiber 2g) **Exchanges:** ½ Starch, 3 Other Carbohydrate, 2 Fat **Carbohydrate Choices:** 4

 Pie Tip Dried Mission figs can be used in place of the dried Calimyrna figs in this tart. Mission figs are darker in color and are not quite as sweet as Calimyrna figs.

cherry-cranberry pie

Prep Time: 15 Minutes * Start to Finish: 2 Hours * 8 servings

CRUST

1 box (15 oz) Pillsbury refrigerated pie crusts, softened as directed on box

FILLING

1 can (21 oz) cherry pie filling

1 can (16 oz) whole berry cranberry sauce

3 tablespoons cornstarch

¼ teaspoon ground cinnamon

GLAZE

½ cup powdered sugar

1 tablespoon light corn syrup

2 to 3 teaspoons water

¼ cup sliced almonds, if desired

1 Heat oven to 425°F. Make pie crust as directed on box for Two-Crust Pie, using 9-inch glass pie plate.

2 In large bowl, mix filling ingredients. Spoon into crust-lined pie plate. Top with second crust; seal edge and flute. Cut slits or shapes in several places in top crust.

3 Bake 35 to 45 minutes or until crust is golden brown. Cover crust edge with foil after 10 to 15 minutes of baking to prevent excessive browning.

4 Remove pie from oven. Immediately, in small bowl, mix powdered sugar, corn syrup and enough water for desired drizzling consistency. Drizzle glaze over hot pie. Sprinkle with almonds. Cool on cooling rack at least 1 hour before serving.

High Altitude (3500–6500 ft): No change.

1 Serving: Calories 340; Total Fat 7g (Saturated Fat 2.5g; Trans Fat 0g); Cholesterol 0mg; Sodium 125mg; Total Carbohydrate 68g (Dietary Fiber 1g) **Exchanges:** 4½ Other Carbohydrate, 1½ Fat **Carbohydrate Choices:** 4½

Pie Tip To get a head start on the holiday rush, you can bake and freeze this pie for up to 2 months. Bake the pie, but omit the glaze. Place in a freezer container and freeze. To thaw, place the pie in the oven at 325°F for 45 minutes or until warm. Make the glaze and immediately spread over the warm pie; sprinkle with almonds.

cranberry mousse mini tarts

Prep Time: 45 Minutes ✳ Start to Finish: 2 Hours 5 Minutes ✳ 24 mini tarts

FILLING
⅔ cup water

1 envelope unflavored gelatin

½ cup granulated sugar

1 cup whole cranberries, chopped

½ teaspoon grated orange peel

CRUST
1 box (15 oz) Pillsbury refrigerated pie crusts, softened as directed on box

Coarse sugar, if desired

TOPPING
¼ cup whipping cream

3 teaspoons powdered sugar

1 In small bowl, place water. Sprinkle gelatin over water; let stand 15 minutes to soften. In 1½-quart saucepan, heat ½ cup granulated sugar and the cranberries just to boiling over medium heat, stirring occasionally. Remove from heat; stir in gelatin mixture and orange peel. Refrigerate 30 to 40 minutes or until mixture just starts to thicken.

2 Heat oven to 425°F. Spray 24 miniature muffin cups with cooking spray.

3 Unroll crusts on work surface. With 2½-inch scalloped-edge round cutter, cut 15 rounds from 1 crust and 9 from the other. Fit rounds into muffin cups, pressing in gently. Generously prick crusts with fork. From remaining crust, cut 24 1-inch star shapes; place on ungreased cookie sheet. Sprinkle with coarse sugar. Bake crusts 6 to 9 minutes or until light golden brown. Cool crusts completely on cooling rack, about 15 minutes; remove from muffin cups. Meanwhile, bake star shapes 3 to 4 minutes or until light golden brown.

4 In chilled small bowl, beat whipping cream with electric mixer on high speed until soft peaks form. Add 2 teaspoons of the powdered sugar; beat until stiff peaks form. Fold in cranberry mixture; refrigerate about 10 minutes or until thickened. Spoon about 1 tablespoon mixture into each crust; top each with 1 star. Store in refrigerator. Just before serving, sprinkle with remaining 1 teaspoon powdered sugar.

High Altitude (3500–6500 ft): No change.

1 Mini Tart: Calories 80; Total Fat 3.5g (Saturated Fat 1.5g; Trans Fat 0g); Cholesterol 0mg; Sodium 45mg; Total Carbohydrate 10g (Dietary Fiber 0g) **Exchanges:** ½ Other Carbohydrate, 1 Fat **Carbohydrate Choices:** ½

 Pie Tip These mini tarts are the perfect dessert for a holiday party. Both the tarts and the stars can be made a day ahead of time. Store the tarts in the refrigerator and the stars at room temperature. Just before serving, top each tart with a star and a sprinkle of powdered sugar.

white chocolate–cranberry-pecan tart

Prep Time: 30 Minutes ✳ Start to Finish: 3 Hours 15 Minutes ✳ 12 servings

CRUST
1 Pillsbury refrigerated pie crust (from 15-oz box), softened as directed on box

FILLING
1 cup fresh or frozen cranberries

1 cup pecan halves

1 cup white vanilla baking chips

3 eggs

¾ cup packed brown sugar

¾ cup light corn syrup

2 tablespoons all-purpose flour

1 teaspoon grated orange peel

SERVE WITH, IF DESIRED
Whipped cream

1 Place cookie sheet in oven on middle oven rack. Heat oven to 400°F. Place pie crust in 10-inch tart pan with removable bottom as directed on box for One-Crust Filled Pie.

2 Layer cranberries, pecans and baking chips in crust-lined pan. In large bowl, beat eggs with whisk. Add brown sugar, corn syrup, flour and orange peel; blend well. Pour over cranberry mixture.

3 Place tart on cookie sheet in oven. Bake 25 minutes. Cover tart loosely with foil lightly sprayed with cooking spray. Bake 10 to 20 minutes longer or until crust is golden brown and filling is set in center. Remove foil; cool completely on cooling rack, about 2 hours. To remove tart from sides of pan, place the pan on a wide, short can and pull down the side of the pan (see page 80). If necessary, use a thin-bladed knife to loosen crust from the side of the pan. Serve with whipped cream. Cover and refrigerate any remaining tart.

High Altitude (3500–6500 ft): In step 3, after adding foil, bake 10 to 15 minutes longer.

1 Serving: Calories 390; Total Fat 17g (Saturated Fat 7g; Trans Fat 0g); Cholesterol 55mg; Sodium 160mg; Total Carbohydrate 54g (Dietary Fiber 1g) **Exchanges:** 1 Starch, 2½ Other Carbohydrate, 3½ Fat **Carbohydrate Choices:** 3½

chocolate-cranberry-pecan tart: Substitute 1 cup semisweet chocolate chips for the vanilla baking chips. In chilled small bowl, beat 1 cup whipping cream, ¼ cup sugar and 2 tablespoons unsweetened baking cocoa with electric mixer on high speed until soft peaks form. Serve with tart.

Pie Tip If you don't have a 10-inch tart pan, you can make this dessert in a 9-inch glass pie plate. When mixing the filling, increase the flour to 3 tablespoons.

irish cream–chocolate tart

Prep Time: 15 Minutes ✳ Start to Finish: 4 Hours 5 Minutes ✳ 12 servings

CRUST

1 Pillsbury refrigerated pie crust (from 15-oz box), softened as directed on box

FILLING

1½ cups semisweet chocolate chips

1 can (14 oz) sweetened condensed milk

⅓ cup Irish cream liqueur or whipping cream

2 eggs

TOPPING

½ cup powdered sugar

⅓ cup unsweetened baking cocoa

Dash salt

1½ cups whipping cream

1 teaspoon vanilla

Additional unsweetened baking cocoa, if desired

White chocolate curls, if desired

1 Heat oven to 425°F. Place pie crust in 9-inch springform pan; press in bottom and 1½ inches up side of pan. Bake 9 to 11 minutes or until golden brown. Cool completely on cooling rack, about 15 minutes.

2 In medium microwavable bowl, microwave chocolate chips on High 40 seconds. Stir; microwave 5 to 15 seconds longer, stirring after every 5 seconds, or until chocolate is melted and smooth. Cool 3 minutes.

3 In large bowl, beat condensed milk, liqueur, eggs and melted chocolate with electric mixer on medium speed until smooth. Pour into cooled baked crust.

4 Bake 15 minutes. Reduce oven temperature to 350°F. Bake 20 to 30 minutes longer or until center is set. Cool completely on cooling rack, about 1 hour. Refrigerate 2 hours.

5 In medium bowl, beat all topping ingredients except additional cocoa and chocolate curls with electric mixer on high speed until stiff peaks form. Spread topping evenly over tart. To remove tart from sides of pan, place the pan on a wide, short can and pull down the side of the pan (see page 80). If necessary, use a thin-bladed knife to loosen crust from the side of the pan. Sprinkle with additional cocoa and garnish with chocolate curls. Store in refrigerator until ready to serve. Cover and refrigerate any remaining tart.

High Altitude (3500–6500 ft): Place pan of water on oven rack below the rack tart will be baked on. In step 3, add ¼ cup all-purpose flour to ingredients in bowl. In step 4, increase second bake time at 350°F to 25 to 35 minutes.

1 Serving: Calories 440; Total Fat 25g (Saturated Fat 14g; Trans Fat 0g); Cholesterol 85mg; Sodium 150mg; Total Carbohydrate 48g (Dietary Fiber 2g) **Exchanges:** ½ Starch, 2½ Other Carbohydrate, ½ Medium-Fat Meat, 4½ Fat **Carbohydrate Choices:** 3

Pie Tip Top this chocolate tart with fresh raspberries or sliced strawberries. To make it extra-special, garnish it with white chocolate curls and fresh mint leaves. Make the curls by pulling a vegetable peeler toward you across a white baking bar. Press firmly, using long, thin strokes.

bittersweet chocolate tart with kiwifruit

Prep Time: 35 Minutes ✳ Start to Finish: 2 Hours ✳ 12 servings

CRUST

1 Pillsbury refrigerated pie crust (from 15-oz box), softened as directed on box

FILLING

6 oz bittersweet baking chocolate, chopped

6 tablespoons butter or margarine

2 tablespoons milk

2 tablespoons corn syrup

½ teaspoon vanilla

4 eggs

SERVE WITH

1 cup sweetened whipped cream

2 kiwifruit, peeled, sliced

1 Heat oven to 450°F. Bake pie crust as directed on box for One-Crust Baked Shell, using 10-inch tart pan with removable bottom or 9-inch glass pie plate. Cool completely on cooling rack, about 15 minutes. Reduce oven temperature to 325°F.

2 In 2-quart saucepan, melt chocolate and butter over low heat, stirring until smooth. Set aside to cool slightly.

3 In medium bowl, beat remaining filling ingredients with whisk. Gradually add egg mixture to chocolate mixture, whisking until well combined. Pour into partially baked crust.

4 Bake at 325°F 15 to 20 minutes or until set. Cool completely on cooling rack, about 45 minutes. To remove tart from sides of pan, place the pan on a wide, short can and pull down the side of the pan (see page 80). If necessary, use a thin-bladed knife to loosen crust from the side of the pan. Serve with whipped cream and kiwifruit. Cover and refrigerate any remaining tart.

High Altitude (3500–6500 ft): No change.

1 Serving: Calories 300; Total Fat 23g (Saturated Fat 12g; Trans Fat 0g); Cholesterol 100mg; Sodium 150mg; Total Carbohydrate 18g (Dietary Fiber 3g) **Exchanges:** 1 Starch, 4½ Fat **Carbohydrate Choices:** 1

Pie Tip Bittersweet chocolate is similar to semisweet chocolate, but it contains more chocolate liquor (the paste that comes from ground cocoa beans) and less sugar. Bittersweet and semi-sweet chocolates can be used interchangeably in this tart.

eggnog pie

Prep Time: 45 Minutes ✳ Start to Finish: 4 Hours 45 Minutes ✳ 10 servings

CRUST

1 Pillsbury refrigerated pie crust (from 15-oz box), softened as directed on package

FILLING

1½ cups dairy eggnog (do not use canned)

1 envelope unflavored gelatin

1 cup powdered sugar

¼ cup butter or margarine, softened

2 packages (8 oz each) cream cheese, softened

¼ teaspoon ground nutmeg

½ teaspoon rum extract

SERVE WITH, IF DESIRED

Sweetened whipped cream

Ground nutmeg

1 Heat oven to 450°F. Bake pie crust as directed on box for One-Crust Baked Shell, using 9-inch glass pie plate. Cool completely on cooling rack, about 15 minutes.

2 In 1-quart saucepan, place 1 cup of the eggnog. Sprinkle gelatin evenly over eggnog; let stand 1 minute to soften. Cook over medium heat, stirring constantly, until gelatin is dissolved. Remove from heat; set aside.

3 In large bowl, beat powdered sugar, butter and cream cheese with electric mixer on low speed until light and fluffy. Gradually beat in nutmeg, rum extract, gelatin mixture and remaining ½ cup eggnog. Beat on high speed until smooth. Refrigerate about 15 minutes or until mixture mounds slightly when stirred.

4 Pour filling into cooled baked crust. Refrigerate pie until firm, about 4 hours. To serve, top each serving with whipped cream and a sprinkle of nutmeg. Cover and refrigerate any remaining pie.

High Altitude (3500–6500 ft): No change.

1 Serving: Calories 370; Total Fat 27g (Saturated Fat 15g; Trans Fat 0.5g); Cholesterol 90mg; Sodium 280mg; Total Carbohydrate 26g (Dietary Fiber 0g) **Exchanges:** 2 Starch, 5 Fat **Carbohydrate Choices:** 2

Pie Tip Raspberry sauce would be lovely served with this eggnog pie. In 1-quart saucepan, mix 3 tablespoons sugar and 2 teaspoons cornstarch. Stir in ⅓ cup water and 1 box (10 oz) frozen raspberries in syrup, thawed and undrained. Cook over medium heat, stirring constantly, until mixture thickens and boils; boil 1 minute. Strain sauce to remove seeds if desired. Cover and refrigerate up to 10 days. To serve, top each serving with whipped cream and drizzle with sauce.

streusel-topped pear-cranberry tart

Prep Time: 25 Minutes ❋ Start to Finish: 1 Hour 20 Minutes ❋ 8 servings

CRUST

1 Pillsbury refrigerated pie crust (from 15-oz box), softened as directed on box

FILLING

½ cup sugar

4 teaspoons cornstarch

2 teaspoons ground cinnamon

4 cups thinly sliced, peeled pears (4 to 5 medium)

¾ cup fresh or frozen (thawed) cranberries

STREUSEL

¼ cup sugar

¼ cup all-purpose flour

2 tablespoons butter or margarine, softened

GARNISH, IF DESIRED

Additional fresh cranberries

Mint leaves

1 Place cookie sheet in oven on middle rack. Heat oven to 375°F. Place pie crust in 10-inch tart pan with removable bottom or 9-inch glass pie plate as directed on box for One-Crust Filled Pie.

2 In large bowl, mix ½ cup sugar, the cornstarch and cinnamon. Gently stir in pears and cranberries until evenly coated. Spoon mixture into crust-lined pan.

3 In small bowl, mix ¼ cup sugar and the flour. Cut in butter, using pastry blender (or fork or pulling 2 table knives through mixture in opposite directions), until mixture looks like coarse crumbs. Sprinkle evenly over filling.

4 Place tart on cookie sheet in oven. Bake 45 to 55 minutes or until crust is deep golden brown and pears are tender. To remove tart from sides of pan, place the pan on a wide, short can and pull down the side of the pan (see page 80). If necessary, use a thin-bladed knife to loosen crust from the side of the pan. Serve warm or cool. Garnish with fresh cranberries and mint leaves.

High Altitude (3500–6500 ft): No change.

1 Serving: Calories 290; Total Fat 10g (Saturated Fat 4.5g; Trans Fat 0g); Cholesterol 10mg; Sodium 130mg; Total Carbohydrate 48g (Dietary Fiber 3g) **Exchanges:** 3 Other Carbohydrate, 2 Fat **Carbohydrate Choices:** 3

Pie Tip Fresh cranberries are available November through December. These ruby-red berries freeze well for up to 1 year in the original plastic bag.

pear-cranberry pie with eggnog sauce

Prep Time: 25 Minutes ✳ Start to Finish: 2 Hours 25 Minutes ✳ 8 servings

CRUST

1 Pillsbury refrigerated pie crust (from 15-oz box), softened as directed on box

FILLING

2 ripe medium pears, peeled, cut into ¼-inch slices

1 cup fresh cranberries

½ cup sugar

¼ teaspoon ground nutmeg

½ cup sour cream

3 eggs

SAUCE

1 teaspoon cornstarch

1 cup dairy eggnog (do not use canned)

1 tablespoon light rum or ½ teaspoon rum extract

1 Heat oven to 425°F. Bake pie crust as directed on box for One-Crust Baked Shell, using 9-inch glass pie plate. Cool on cooling rack 5 minutes.

2 Reduce oven temperature to 350°F. Layer pear slices and cranberries in crust.

3 In medium bowl, beat sugar, nutmeg, sour cream and eggs with whisk until smooth and well blended. Pour evenly over fruit.

4 Bake 15 minutes. Cover crust edge with strips of foil to prevent excessive browning. Bake 40 to 45 minutes longer or until custard is just set and pears are fork-tender. Cool completely on cooling rack, about 1 hour.

5 In 1-quart saucepan, mix cornstarch with 1 tablespoon of the eggnog until mixture is smooth. With whisk, beat in remaining eggnog; cook over medium heat 6 to 8 minutes, stirring constantly, until mixture just begins to boil. Remove from heat; stir in rum. Serve warm sauce with pie. Refrigerate any remaining pie and sauce.

High Altitude (3500–6500 ft): No change.

1 Serving: Calories 280; Total Fat 13g (Saturated Fat 5g; Trans Fat 0g); Cholesterol 115mg; Sodium 160mg; Total Carbohydrate 36g (Dietary Fiber 2g) **Exchanges:** 1 Starch, 1½ Other Carbohydrate, 2½ Fat **Carbohydrate Choices:** 2½

 You can make this pie in a 9-inch tart pan with removable bottom. Because the sides of the tart pan are not as high as a pie plate, place a cookie sheet or piece of foil on the rack under the rack the tart is on before baking to catch any drips. Bake 50 to 55 minutes.

classic pecan pie

Prep Time: 15 Minutes ✳ Start to Finish: 3 Hours 10 Minutes ✳ 8 servings

CRUST
1 Pillsbury refrigerated pie
    crust (from 15-oz box),
    softened as directed on box

All-purpose flour

FILLING
3 eggs

1 cup sugar

1 cup corn syrup

2 tablespoons butter or
    margarine, melted

1 teaspoon vanilla

1½ cups pecan halves

1 Heat oven to 350°F. Unroll crust on work surface. Sprinkle both sides of crust with flour. Place crust in 9-inch glass pie plate as directed on box for One-Crust Filled Pie.

2 In medium bowl, beat eggs slightly with whisk. Add sugar, corn syrup, butter and vanilla; stir until well blended. Stir in pecans. Pour mixture into crust-lined pie plate. Cover crust edge with foil to prevent excessive browning.

3 Bake 50 to 55 minutes or until filling is set around edge and slightly soft in center, removing foil during last 15 minutes of bake time. Cool completely on cooling rack, about 2 hours 30 minutes. Refrigerate until ready to serve. Cover and refrigerate any remaining pie.

High Altitude (3500–6500 ft): No change.

1 Serving: Calories 540; Total Fat 25g (Saturated Fat 6g; Trans Fat 0g); Cholesterol 90mg; Sodium 200mg; Total Carbohydrate 74g (Dietary Fiber 2g) **Exchanges:** 1 Starch, 4 Other Carbohydrate, 5 Fat **Carbohydrate Choices:** 5

california pecan pie: Stir ¼ cup sour cream into eggs until blended.

kentucky bourbon pecan pie: Add up to 2 tablespoons bourbon to filling.

chocolate pecan pie: Decrease sugar to ⅓ cup. Melt four 1-oz squares semisweet baking chocolate with the butter.

coconut-pecan chocolate pie

Prep Time: 25 Minutes ✳ Start to Finish: 2 Hours 45 Minutes ✳ 8 servings

CRUST

1 Pillsbury refrigerated pie crust (from 15-oz box), softened as directed on box

All-purpose flour

1 cup coconut

½ cup chopped pecans

FILLING

1 cup sugar

⅓ cup butter or margarine

4 oz sweet baking chocolate, chopped

3 tablespoons all-purpose flour

½ cup evaporated milk or half-and-half

1 teaspoon vanilla

4 eggs

SERVE WITH, IF DESIRED

Whipped cream

Coconut, toasted*

1 Heat oven to 350°F. Unroll pie crust on work surface. Sprinkle both sides of crust with flour. Place crust in 9-inch glass pie plate as directed on box for One-Crust Filled Pie. Sprinkle coconut and pecans in bottom of crust-lined pie plate.

2 In 2-quart saucepan, heat sugar, butter and chocolate over low heat, stirring constantly, until smooth. Pour chocolate mixture into medium bowl; cool 5 minutes. Beat in 3 tablespoons flour with whisk until well combined. Beat in evaporated milk, vanilla and eggs until well blended.

3 Slowly pour chocolate mixture over coconut and pecans. Cover crust edge with foil to prevent excessive browning.

4 Bake 40 to 50 minutes or until center is set, removing foil during last 15 minutes of bake time. Cool on cooling rack at least 1 hour 30 minutes. Serve with whipped cream and toasted coconut. Cover and refrigerate any remaining pie.

∗To toast coconut, sprinkle in ungreased heavy skillet. Cook over medium-low heat 6 to 14 minutes, stirring frequently until browning begins, then stirring constantly until golden brown. Or spread in thin layer in microwavable glass pie plate. Microwave on Medium 4½ to 8 minutes until light golden brown, tossing with fork after each minute.

High Altitude (3500–6500 ft): No change.

1 Serving: Calories 430; Total Fat 31g (Saturated Fat 15g; Trans Fat 0g); Cholesterol 135mg; Sodium 240mg; Total Carbohydrate 32g (Dietary Fiber 2g) **Exchanges:** 2 Other Carbohydrate, 1 High-Fat Meat, 4½ Fat **Carbohydrate Choices:** 2

Pie Tip Other chopped nuts such as walnuts or almonds can be used instead of the pecans. You may want to add ½ teaspoon almond extract to the filling if you use almonds.

coffee-pecan tarts

Prep Time: 25 Minutes ✳ Start to Finish: 1 Hour 15 Minutes ✳ 4 tarts

CRUST

1 Pillsbury refrigerated pie crust (from 15-oz box), softened as directed on box

4 foil tart pans (4½ to 5 inch)

Coarse sugar or granulated sugar

FILLING

1 egg

¼ cup granulated sugar

¼ cup light corn syrup

2 tablespoons coffee-flavored liqueur or cold strong coffee

Dash salt

½ teaspoon vanilla

½ cup pecan halves

SERVE WITH, IF DESIRED

½ cup whipped cream or whipped topping

1 Heat oven to 375°F. On lightly floured surface, unroll crust. With 4½-inch round cookie cutter, cut 4 rounds from crust. Fit rounds in bottom and ½ inch up sides of foil tart pans. Prick bottoms and sides generously with fork. Place pans on ungreased cookie sheet.

2 Cut small star shapes from remaining pie crust pieces; place on same cookie sheet with tart pans. Prick stars with fork; sprinkle lightly with coarse sugar.

3 Bake tart shells and stars 6 to 8 minutes or just until shells are dry and stars are golden brown.

4 Meanwhile, in medium bowl, beat egg with whisk. Beat in ¼ cup granulated sugar, the corn syrup, liqueur, salt and vanilla.

5 Remove partially baked tart shells and baked stars from oven. Remove stars from cookie sheet. Arrange pecans evenly in tart shells. Pour egg mixture evenly over pecans. Return tarts to oven; bake 16 to 20 minutes longer or until crusts are golden brown and center is set. Cool completely on cooling rack, about 30 minutes.

6 Remove tarts from pans. To serve, top each tart with whipped cream, and garnish with pie crust stars.

High Altitude (3500–6500 ft): In step 3, bake tart shells and stars 8 to 10 minutes. In step 4, add 1 tablespoon all-purpose flour to egg mixture. In step 5, bake tarts 16 to 18 minutes.

1 Tart: Calories 480; Total Fat 24g (Saturated Fat 6g; Trans Fat 0g); Cholesterol 60mg; Sodium 300mg; Total Carbohydrate 61g (Dietary Fiber 1g) **Exchanges:** 1 Starch, 3 Other Carbohydrate, 4½ Fat **Carbohydrate Choices:** 4

Pie Tip If you don't have a 4½-inch round cookie cutter, use the top of a 4½-inch diameter bowl as a pattern. Place the bowl upside down on the crust, and cut around the bowl using a sharp paring knife.

pomegranate tartlets

Prep Time: 45 Minutes ✳ Start to Finish: 1 Hour 45 Minutes ✳ 36 tartlets

CRUST
3 Pillsbury refrigerated pie crusts (from two 15-oz boxes), softened as directed on box

FILLING
1 pomegranate

1 box (4-serving size) vanilla pudding and pie filling mix (not instant)

1¾ cups whipping cream

2 tablespoons dark rum or ½ teaspoon rum extract

TOPPING
1 teaspoon powdered sugar

1 Heat oven to 450°F. Unroll pie crusts on work surface. With 2½-inch plain- or scalloped-edge round cutter, cut crusts into 36 rounds. Fit rounds into ungreased miniature muffin cups, pressing in gently (see photo). Generously prick crusts with fork.

2 Bake 7 to 9 minutes or until light golden brown. Remove tartlet shells from muffin cups; place on cooling racks. Cool 10 minutes.

3 Meanwhile, cut pomegranate in half; remove seeds. Set aside.

4 In 2-quart saucepan, stir pudding mix and whipping cream with whisk until blended. Cook over medium heat about 5 minutes or until mixture comes to a boil, stirring constantly. Remove from heat; stir in rum.

5 Immediately spoon about 2 rounded teaspoons filling into each tartlet shell. Top each with about 1 teaspoon pomegranate seeds. Cover loosely; refrigerate at least 1 hour or until serving time. Just before serving, sprinkle tartlets with powdered sugar.

High Altitude (3500–6500 ft): No change.

1 Tartlet: Calories 90; Total Fat 6g (Saturated Fat 3g; Trans Fat 0g); Cholesterol 15mg; Sodium 60mg; Total Carbohydrate 8g (Dietary Fiber 0g) **Exchanges:** ½ Other Carbohydrate, 1½ Fat **Carbohydrate Choices:** ½

Shaping Tartlet Crust

Gently press rounds, pleating slightly to fit, into mini muffin cups.

Pie Tip To remove the seeds from a pomegranate, you'll need a sharp knife and bowl of cold water. Score the pomegranate skin from top to bottom about 5 times, evenly spaced. Hold the pomegranate under water in the bowl, and pull it apart into sections. Remove the seeds with your fingers or a small spoon while holding it under water. The seeds will sink to the bottom, and the skin and membrane will float to the top. Remove the membrane with your fingers, and drain the seeds in a strainer.

peppermint candy tarts

Prep Time: 45 Minutes ✳ Start to Finish: 2 Hours 10 Minutes ✳ 30 tarts

CRUST
1 box (15 oz) Pillsbury
 refrigerated pie crusts,
 softened as directed on box

FILLING
2 cups powdered sugar

3 tablespoons butter or
 margarine, softened

2 or 3 drops red food color

2 to 3 tablespoons milk

½ cup crushed red and white
 hard peppermint candies
 (about 18 candies)

1 Heat oven to 425°F. Spray 30 miniature muffin cups with cooking spray.

2 Unroll crusts on work surface. With 2½-inch scalloped- or plain-edge round cutter, cut 15 rounds from each crust. Fit rounds into muffin cups, pressing in gently. Prick crusts generously with fork.

3 Bake 6 to 9 minutes or until light golden brown. Cool completely on cooling rack, about 15 minutes. Remove tarts from muffin cups.

4 In small bowl, beat filling ingredients except crushed candies with electric mixer on medium speed until smooth and creamy. Stir in ¼ cup of the candies. Spoon or pipe 1 heaping measuring teaspoon filling into center of each tart shell. Sprinkle with remaining crushed candies.

High Altitude (3500–6500 ft): No change.

1 Tart: Calories 130; Total Fat 4g (Saturated Fat 2.5g; Trans Fat 0g); Cholesterol 15mg; Sodium 60mg; Total Carbohydrate 21g (Dietary Fiber 0g) **Exchanges:** 1½ Other Carbohydrate, 1 Fat **Carbohydrate Choices:** 1½

Pie Tip For the holidays, try green food color to make the filling green, and use crushed green and white hard peppermint candies for the topping. Be extra festive and make batches of both colors!

peppermint truffle pie

Prep Time: 20 Minutes * Start to Finish: 8 Hours 30 Minutes * 12 servings

FILLING

1 bag (12 oz) semisweet chocolate chips (2 cups)

1 cup half-and-half

¼ cup butter or margarine, cut into pieces

1½ teaspoons peppermint extract

CRUST

1 Pillsbury refrigerated pie crust (from 15-oz box), softened as directed on box

TOPPING

1 cup white vanilla baking chips

1½ cups whipping cream

12 red and white hard peppermint candies

1 Heat oven to 450°F. In medium microwavable bowl, place chocolate chips, half-and-half and butter. Microwave on High 2 minutes to 2 minutes 30 seconds or until melted, stirring once or twice. Stir in peppermint extract. Beat with electric mixer or whisk until well blended. Refrigerate 45 to 60 minutes or until thickened.

2 Meanwhile, bake pie crust as directed on box for One-Crust Baked Shell, using 9-inch glass pie plate.

3 In small microwavable bowl, place white vanilla baking chips and whipping cream. Microwave on High 1 minute 30 seconds or until smooth, stirring once or twice. Cover and refrigerate until chilled, about 2 hours.

4 Pour semisweet chocolate mixture into cooled baked crust. Reserve 3 peppermint candies. Crush remaining candies, and sprinkle over chocolate. Refrigerate until firm, about 2 hours.

5 In medium bowl, beat vanilla mixture with electric mixer on high speed until light and fluffy. Do not overbeat. Carefully spoon and spread evenly over chocolate. Refrigerate until firm, at least 4 hours. Just before serving, garnish with peppermint candies. Cover and refrigerate any remaining pie.

High Altitude (3500–6500 ft): No change.

1 Serving: Calories 530; Total Fat 36g (Saturated Fat 21g; Trans Fat 0.5g); Cholesterol 55mg; Sodium 140mg; Total Carbohydrate 47g (Dietary Fiber 2g) **Exchanges:** ½ Starch, 2½ Other Carbohydrate, ½ Medium-Fat Meat, 6½ Fat **Carbohydrate Choices:** 3

 This pie can be made and stored in the refrigerator up to 24 hours before serving, which makes it ideal for the holidays.

pumpkin pie

Prep Time: 25 Minutes ✳ Start to Finish: 4 Hours ✳ 8 servings

CRUST

1 Pillsbury refrigerated pie crust (from 15-oz box), softened as directed on box

FILLING

¾ cup sugar

1½ teaspoons pumpkin pie spice

½ teaspoon salt

1 can (15 oz) pumpkin (not pumpkin pie mix)

1 can (12 oz) evaporated milk

2 eggs, beaten

SERVE WITH, IF DESIRED

Sweetened whipped cream or frozen whipped topping, thawed

1 Heat oven to 425°F. Place pie crust in 9-inch glass pie plate as directed on box for One-Crust Filled Pie.

2 In large bowl, beat filling ingredients with hand beater or whisk until well blended. Pour into crust-lined pie plate. Cover crust edge with foil to prevent excessive browning.

3 Bake 15 minutes. Reduce oven temperature to 350°F; bake 40 to 50 minutes longer or until knife inserted near center comes out clean. Cool on cooling rack 30 minutes. Refrigerate at least 2 hours before serving. Serve with whipped cream. Cover and refrigerate any remaining pie.

High Altitude (3500–6500 ft): No change.

1 Serving: Calories 290; Total Fat 12g (Saturated Fat 5g; Trans Fat 0g); Cholesterol 70mg; Sodium 320mg; Total Carbohydrate 41g (Dietary Fiber 1g) **Exchanges:** ½ Starch, 1 Other Carbohydrate, 2½ Fat **Carbohydrate Choices:** 3

creme pumpkin pie: Bake and cool pie as directed above. In small bowl, beat 1 package (3 oz) cream cheese, softened, 2 teaspoons milk and 1 teaspoon grated orange peel until smooth. Gently fold in 1 container (8 oz) frozen whipped topping, thawed. Spoon over pie; cover and refrigerate until serving and any remaining pie.

eggnog pumpkin pie: Substitute 1½ cups dairy eggnog for the evaporated milk.

 For easy holiday entertaining, you can bake this pie up to 3 days before serving. After pie is cooled, cover and refrigerate until ready to serve.

maple-walnut-pumpkin pie

Prep Time: 20 Minutes ✳ Start to Finish: 3 Hours ✳ 8 servings

CRUST

1 Pillsbury refrigerated pie
  crust (from 15-oz box),
  softened as directed on box

FILLING

1 can (15 oz) pumpkin (not
  pumpkin pie mix)

1 can (14 oz) sweetened
  condensed milk (not
  evaporated)

2 tablespoons real maple
  syrup or maple-flavored
  syrup

1½ teaspoons pumpkin pie
  spice

2 eggs

STREUSEL

¼ cup packed brown sugar

2 tablespoons all-purpose
  flour

2 tablespoons cold butter or
  margarine

¼ cup finely chopped walnuts

TOPPING

1 cup whipping cream

2 tablespoons packed brown
  sugar

Chopped walnuts, if desired

1 Heat oven to 425°F. Place pie crust in 9-inch glass pie plate as directed on box for One-Crust Filled Pie. In large bowl, beat filling ingredients with electric mixer until smooth. Pour into crust-lined pie plate. Bake 10 minutes.

2 Meanwhile, in small bowl, mix ¼ cup brown sugar and the flour. Cut in butter, using pastry blender (or fork or pulling 2 table knives through mixture in opposite directions), until mixture looks like coarse crumbs. Stir in nuts; set aside.

3 Remove pie from oven. Reduce oven temperature to 350°F. Sprinkle streusel over pie. Cover crust edge with foil to prevent excessive browning.

4 Return to oven; bake 30 to 35 minutes longer or until knife inserted 1 inch from edge comes out clean. Cool completely on cooling rack, about 2 hours. Serve or refrigerate until serving time.

5 Just before serving, in chilled medium bowl, beat whipping cream and 2 tablespoons brown sugar with electric mixer on medium-high speed until soft peaks form. Serve pie with whipped cream and chopped walnuts. Cover and refrigerate any remaining pie.

High Altitude (3500–6500 ft): In step 4, bake 40 to 45 minutes.

1 Serving: Calories 520; Total Fat 27g (Saturated Fat 13g; Trans Fat 0.5g); Cholesterol 115mg; Sodium 230mg; Total Carbohydrate 61g (Dietary Fiber 2g) **Exchanges:** 2 Starch, 2 Other Carbohydrate, 5 Fat **Carbohydrate Choices:** 4

 Pie Tip Be sure to purchase plain pumpkin, not pumpkin pie mix, which includes seasonings—and canned sweetened condensed milk, which is thick and sweet, rather than canned evaporated milk, which is usually used when making pumpkin pie.

streusel pumpkin pie

Prep Time: 20 Minutes ✳ Start to Finish: 2 Hours 5 Minutes ✳ 8 servings

CRUST

1 Pillsbury refrigerated pie crust (from 15-oz box), softened as directed on box

FILLING

1 can (15 oz) pumpkin (not pumpkin pie mix)

1 can (12 oz) evaporated milk

½ cup granulated sugar

2 eggs, slightly beaten

1½ teaspoons pumpkin pie spice

¼ teaspoon salt

STREUSEL

¼ cup packed brown sugar

2 tablespoons all-purpose flour

2 tablespoons cold butter or margarine

½ cup chopped pecans

TOPPING

1 teaspoon grated orange peel

1 container (8 oz) frozen whipped topping, thawed

1 Heat oven to 425°F. Make pie crust as directed on box for One-Crust Filled Pie, using 9-inch glass pie plate.

2 In large bowl, mix filling ingredients until well blended. Pour into crust-lined pie plate.

3 Bake 15 minutes. Reduce oven temperature to 350°F. Bake 15 minutes longer.

4 Meanwhile, in small bowl, mix brown sugar and flour. Cut in butter, using pastry blender (or fork or pulling 2 table knives through mixture in opposite directions), until mixture looks like coarse crumbs. Stir in pecans. Sprinkle streusel over pumpkin filling. Bake 15 to 20 minutes longer or until knife inserted in center comes out clean. Cool completely on cooling rack, about 1 hour.

5 Gently fold orange peel into whipped topping. Serve topping with pie. Cover and refrigerate any remaining pie and topping.

High Altitude (3500–6500 ft): Before baking, cover crust edge with foil to prevent excessive browning. Bake 15 minutes. Reduce oven temperature to 350°F. Bake 15 minutes longer. Meanwhile, in small bowl, mix streusel ingredients. Remove pie from oven. Remove foil; sprinkle streusel over pumpkin filling. Return to oven; bake 20 to 30 minutes longer.

1 Serving: Calories 440; Total Fat 23g (Saturated Fat 11g; Trans Fat 0g); Cholesterol 70mg; Sodium 280mg; Total Carbohydrate 51g (Dietary Fiber 3g) **Exchanges:** 2 Starch, 1½ Other Carbohydrate, 4½ Fat **Carbohydrate Choices:** 3½

jack-o'-lantern orange-pumpkin pie

Prep Time: 20 Minutes ✳ Start to Finish: 2 Hours 20 Minutes ✳ 8 servings

CRUST

1 Pillsbury refrigerated pie
crust (from 15-oz box),
softened as directed on box

FILLING

¾ cup sugar

1½ teaspoons pumpkin pie
spice*

½ teaspoon salt

1 can (15 oz) pumpkin (not
pumpkin pie mix)

1 can (12 oz) evaporated milk

2 teaspoons grated orange
peel

2 eggs, beaten

TOPPING

¾ cup sour cream

2 tablespoons sugar

2 teaspoons frozen orange
juice concentrate, thawed

3 drops orange gel food color

DRIZZLE

2 tablespoons semisweet
chocolate chips

1½ teaspoons whipping cream

1 Heat oven to 425°F. Place pie crust in ungreased 9-inch glass pie plate as
directed on box for One-Crust Filled Pie.

2 In large bowl, mix filling ingredients. Pour into crust-lined pie plate. Cover
crust edge with foil to prevent excessive browning. Bake 15 minutes.
Reduce oven temperature to 350°F. Bake about 40 minutes or until knife
inserted near center comes out clean; remove foil. Cool on cooling rack
10 minutes.

3 Meanwhile, in small bowl, mix topping ingredients. Spread evenly over
warm pie. Bake 5 minutes longer. Cool completely on cooling rack, about
1 hour.

4 In small resealable freezer plastic bag, place drizzle ingredients; seal bag.
Microwave on Medium about 10 seconds or until softened. Gently squeeze
bag until mixture is smooth. If necessary, continue to microwave in
10-second increments. Cut off tiny corner of bag. Squeeze bag over top of
pie to draw a jack-o'-lantern face. Cover and refrigerate any remaining pie.

✳A mixture of ½ teaspoon each of ground cinnamon, nutmeg and ginger can be substituted
for the 1½ teaspoons pumpkin pie spice.

High Altitude (3500–6500 ft): In step 2, for second bake time, bake about
55 minutes.

1 Serving: Calories 360; Total Fat 17g (Saturated Fat 8g; Trans Fat 0g); Cholesterol 85mg; Sodium
330mg; Total Carbohydrate 47g (Dietary Fiber 2g) **Exchanges:** 1½ Starch, 1½ Other Carbohydrate, 3½ Fat
Carbohydrate Choices: 3

Pie Tip When grating the orange, choose a grater with tiny cutting
edges. Press firmly, but not so hard that you cut into the
bitter white part of the skin.

sweet potato pie

Prep Time: 20 Minutes ✳ Start to Finish: 2 Hours ✳ 8 servings

CRUST

1 Pillsbury refrigerated pie crust (from 15-oz box), softened as directed on box

FILLING

1½ cups mashed canned sweet potatoes

⅔ cup packed brown sugar

1 teaspoon ground cinnamon

½ teaspoon ground allspice

1 cup half-and-half

1 tablespoon dry sherry or lemon juice

2 eggs, beaten

TOPPING

Sweetened whipped cream or whipped topping

1 Heat oven to 425°F. Make pie crust as directed on box for One-Crust Filled Pie, using 9-inch glass pie plate.

2 In medium bowl, mix filling ingredients until smooth. Pour into crust-lined pie plate.

3 Bake 15 minutes. Reduce oven temperature to 350°F. Bake 30 to 40 minutes longer or until center is set. Cool completely on cooling rack, about 45 minutes. Refrigerate until serving. Serve with whipped cream. Cover and refrigerate any remaining pie.

High Altitude (3500–6500 ft): No change.

1 Serving: Calories 300; Total Fat 12g (Saturated Fat 5g; Trans Fat 0g); Cholesterol 70mg; Sodium 160mg; Total Carbohydrate 45g (Dietary Fiber 1g) **Exchanges:** 1 Starch, 2 Other Carbohydrate, 2½ Fat **Carbohydrate Choices:** 3

 Pie Tip For a special touch, pipe the whipped cream onto the pie using a large open star tube. Or save time and use a pressurized can of whipped cream or whipped topping.

pumpkin tart with caramel rum-raisin sauce

Prep Time: 20 Minutes ✳ Start to Finish: 2 Hours 10 Minutes ✳ 12 servings

CRUST
1 Pillsbury refrigerated pie crust (from 15-oz box), softened as directed on box

FILLING
¾ cup sugar

¾ teaspoon ground cinnamon

½ teaspoon ground ginger

⅛ teaspoon ground cloves

½ cup milk

1 can (15 oz) pumpkin (not pumpkin pie mix)

2 eggs

SAUCE
1 cup packed brown sugar

¼ cup whipping cream

¼ cup dark rum*

¼ cup dark corn syrup

½ cup raisins

1 Place cookie sheet in oven on middle rack. Heat oven to 450°F. Place pie crust in 10-inch tart pan with removable bottom as directed on box for One-Crust Filled Pie.

2 In large bowl, mix filling ingredients. Pour into crust-lined pan.

3 Place tart on cookie sheet in oven. Bake 35 to 50 minutes or until crust is deep golden brown. Cool completely on cooling rack, about 1 hour.

4 In 2-quart saucepan, mix sauce ingredients. Cook over medium heat, stirring constantly, until mixture comes to a boil. Reduce heat to low; simmer 5 minutes, stirring constantly. Cool at least 10 minutes before serving. Serve warm sauce with tart. To remove tart from sides of pan, place the pan on a wide, short can and pull down the side of the pan (see page 80). If necessary, use a thin-bladed knife to loosen crust from the side of the pan. Cover and refrigerate any remaining tart and sauce.

✱One and a half teaspoons rum extract plus ¼ cup water can be substituted for dark rum.

High Altitude (3500–6500 ft): In step 3, bake 40 to 50 minutes.

1 Serving: Calories 290; Total Fat 7g (Saturated Fat 3g; Trans Fat 0g); Cholesterol 45mg; Sodium 110mg; Total Carbohydrate 53g (Dietary Fiber 1g) **Exchanges:** ½ Starch, 3 Other Carbohydrate, 1½ Fat **Carbohydrate Choices:** 3½

 Pie Tip If raisins aren't your favorite, just leave them out of the sauce. Or try dried cranberries instead, which would be tasty with this pumpkin tart.

sweet potato pie with streusel topping

Prep Time: 25 Minutes ✳ Start to Finish: 3 Hours 50 Minutes ✳ 8 servings

CRUST
1 Pillsbury refrigerated pie crust (from 15-oz box), softened as directed on box

FILLING
1½ cups mashed cooked dark orange sweet potatoes (about 1 lb uncooked)

½ cup packed brown sugar

2 tablespoons corn syrup

1 cup evaporated milk

3 eggs

1 teaspoon ground cinnamon

½ teaspoon ground nutmeg

⅛ teaspoon ground cloves

⅛ teaspoon ground ginger

STREUSEL
¼ cup packed brown sugar

2 tablespoons all-purpose flour

¼ teaspoon ground cinnamon

2 tablespoons cold butter or margarine

¼ cup chopped pecans

¼ cup chopped walnuts

SERVE WITH, IF DESIRED
1 cup sweetened whipped cream

1 Place cookie sheet in oven on middle rack. Heat oven to 425°F. Place pie crust in 9-inch glass pie plate as directed on box for One-Crust Filled Pie.

2 In large bowl, mix filling ingredients with whisk until smooth; pour into crust-lined pie plate.

3 Place pie on cookie sheet in oven; bake 15 minutes. Reduce oven temperature to 350°F. Bake 20 minutes longer.

4 Meanwhile, in small bowl, mix ¼ cup brown sugar, the flour and ¼ teaspoon cinnamon. Cut in butter, using pastry blender (or fork or pulling 2 table knives through mixture in opposite directions), until mixture looks like coarse crumbs. Stir in pecans and walnuts. Remove pie from oven; carefully sprinkle streusel over filling.

5 Bake 10 to 15 minutes longer or until knife inserted in center comes out clean and streusel is golden brown. Cool completely on cooling rack, about 3 hours. Serve pie with sweetened whipped cream. Cover and refrigerate any remaining pie.

High Altitude (3500–6500 ft): In step 5, bake pie 20 to 25 minutes longer.

1 Serving: Calories 410; Total Fat 18g (Saturated Fat 6g; Trans Fat 0g); Cholesterol 95mg; Sodium 220mg; Total Carbohydrate 54g (Dietary Fiber 3g) **Exchanges:** 1½ Starch, 2 Other Carbohydrate, ½ Medium-Fat Meat, 3 Fat **Carbohydrate Choices:** 3½

Pie Tip If you have pumpkin pie spice on hand, you can use 1¾ teaspoons for the cinnamon, nutmeg, cloves and ginger in the filling.

sweet potato pie with macadamia praline

Prep Time: 25 Minutes ✳ Start to Finish: 2 Hours 25 Minutes ✳ 8 servings

CRUST

1 Pillsbury refrigerated pie crust (from 15-oz box), softened as directed on box

FILLING

¾ cup granulated sugar

1 teaspoon ground cinnamon

½ teaspoon ground ginger

½ teaspoon ground nutmeg

¼ teaspoon salt

1 teaspoon vanilla

1 can (23 oz) sweet potatoes in syrup, drained, mashed (about 2 cups)

1 can (12 oz) evaporated milk

2 eggs, beaten

TOPPING

3 tablespoons packed brown sugar

3 tablespoons corn syrup

1 tablespoon butter or margarine

½ teaspoon vanilla

1 jar (3.5 oz) macadamia nuts, coarsely chopped, or ¾ cup coarsely chopped pecans

SERVE WITH

1 cup crème fraîche or whipped cream

1 Place foil or cookie sheet on oven rack below rack pie will bake on to catch any spills. Heat oven to 425°F. Place pie crust in 9-inch glass pie plate as directed on box for One-Crust Filled Pie.

2 In large bowl, mix filling ingredients. Pour into crust-lined pie plate. Bake 15 minutes. Reduce oven temperature to 350°F. Bake 25 minutes longer.

3 About 5 minutes before end of bake time, in 1-quart saucepan, mix brown sugar, corn syrup and butter. Heat to boiling over low heat. Reduce heat; simmer 2 minutes. Remove from heat; stir in vanilla. Sprinkle nuts evenly over pie. Drizzle with topping mixture.

4 Bake 20 to 30 minutes longer or until knife inserted in center comes out clean. Cover crust edge with strips of foil during last 10 minutes of baking to prevent excessive browning. Cool on cooling rack 1 hour. Serve with crème fraîche. Cover and refrigerate any remaining pie.

High Altitude (3500–6500 ft): No change.

1 Serving: Calories 580; Total Fat 32g (Saturated Fat 13g; Trans Fat 0.5g); Cholesterol 105mg; Sodium 300mg; Total Carbohydrate 67g (Dietary Fiber 3g) **Exchanges:** 1 Starch, 3½ Other Carbohydrate, ½ High-Fat Meat, 5½ Fat **Carbohydrate Choices:** 4½

Pie Tip Crème fraîche is a thick cream that is extremely rich and slightly tangy. Look for it in the dairy section of your supermarket. To make your own, combine 1 cup whipping cream and 3 tablespoons buttermilk. Cover and let stand at room temperature up to 24 hours or until very thick.

raspberry cream heart

Prep Time: 35 Minutes ✳ Start to Finish: 55 Minutes ✳ 8 servings

CRUST

1 box (15 oz) Pillsbury refrigerated pie crusts, softened as directed on box

FILLING

1 package (8 oz) cream cheese, softened

¼ cup powdered sugar

1 jar (14 oz) strawberry pie glaze

TOPPING

2½ cups fresh raspberries

1 teaspoon powdered sugar

1 Heat oven to 450°F. Make paper pattern for 11×10-inch heart. On ungreased cookie sheet, unroll 1 pie crust. With paper pattern as a guide, cut crust into heart shape. Generously prick crust with fork.

2 Bake 8 to 10 minutes or until light golden brown. Cool completely on cooling rack, about 15 minutes. Repeat with second crust.

3 In small bowl, beat cream cheese and ¼ cup powdered sugar with electric mixer on medium speed until smooth. Place 1 cooled baked crust on serving plate. Spread evenly with cream cheese mixture.

4 Reserve ½ cup of the pie glaze. Spread remaining pie glaze over cream cheese mixture. Top with second crust. Spread reserved ½ cup glaze over top crust. Arrange raspberries, stem side down, over top. Sprinkle with 1 teaspoon powdered sugar. Cover and refrigerate any remaining heart.

High Altitude (3500–6500 ft): In step 1, heat oven to 425°F.

1 Serving: Calories 470; Total Fat 26g (Saturated Fat 17g; Trans Fat 0g); Cholesterol 30mg; Sodium 190mg; Total Carbohydrate 55g (Dietary Fiber 2g) **Exchanges:** 1 Starch, 3 Other Carbohydrate, 5 Fat **Carbohydrate Choices:** 3½

Pie Tip Frozen raspberries can be used in place of the fresh berries. And you don't need to thaw them! Just arrange them on the tart 20 minutes before serving.

three-berry cheesecake pie

Prep Time: 45 Minutes ✳ Start to Finish: 4 Hours 35 Minutes ✳ 12 servings

CRUST

1 box (15 oz) Pillsbury refrigerated pie crusts, softened as directed on box

2 tablespoons water

2 tablespoons coarse sugar

FILLING

2 packages (8 oz each) cream cheese, softened

1¼ cups granulated sugar

1 tablespoon lemon juice

1 teaspoon vanilla

1 container (8 oz) frozen whipped topping, thawed

¼ cup seedless raspberry preserves

TOPPING

1 can (21 oz) cherry pie filling

3 cups fresh strawberries, quartered

1 cup fresh raspberries

1 Heat oven to 450°F. Bake 1 pie crust as directed on box for One-Crust Baked Shell, using 10-inch glass pie plate or 10-inch tart pan with removable bottom. Cool completely on cooling rack, about 15 minutes.

2 Meanwhile, spray cookie sheet with cooking spray, or line with cooking parchment paper. Unroll second crust onto cookie sheet. Cut crust into large holly leaves using cookie cutter. Cut small circles for holly berries. Place on cookie sheet; sprinkle with coarse sugar.

3 Bake 8 to 10 minutes or until light golden brown. Carefully remove from cookie sheet to cooling rack. Cool completely, about 15 minutes.

4 In large bowl, beat cream cheese, granulated sugar, lemon juice and vanilla with electric mixer on medium speed until fluffy. Fold in whipped topping until well blended. Spread 2 cups cream cheese mixture in cooled baked crust. Gently spoon and spread preserves over mixture. Spread with remaining cream cheese mixture.

5 In medium bowl, mix pie filling, 2½ cups of the quartered strawberries and ½ cup of the raspberries. Spoon over cream cheese mixture. Sprinkle with remaining strawberries and raspberries. Refrigerate until set, at least 4 hours. Just before serving, arrange some of the holly leaves and berries on cheesecake. Serve individual slices with additional holly leaves and berries. Cover and refrigerate any remaining pie.

High Altitude (3500–6500 ft): No change.

1 Serving: Calories 520; Total Fat 26g (Saturated Fat 15g; Trans Fat 0g); Cholesterol 45mg; Sodium 270mg; Total Carbohydrate 67g (Dietary Fiber 3g) **Exchanges:** ½ Starch, 4 Other Carbohydrate, ½ Medium-Fat Meat, 4½ Fat **Carbohydrate Choices:** 4½

See photo on page 117.

 Be creative and try different berry flavors. Use 1 can (21 oz) raspberry or strawberry pie filling for the cherry pie filling. Or use 1 cup fresh blueberries or blackberries for the raspberries. Any combination of berries will give you a "berry-delicious" pie!

strawberry-kiwi tart

Prep Time: 20 Minutes ✳ Start to Finish: 1 Hour 50 Minutes ✳ 8 servings

CRUST

1 Pillsbury refrigerated pie crust (from 15-oz box), softened as directed on box

FILLING

1½ cups vanilla low-fat yogurt

1 container (8 oz) reduced-fat sour cream

1 box (4-serving size) vanilla instant pudding and pie filling mix

2 tablespoons orange marmalade

TOPPING

1 cup halved fresh strawberries

2 kiwifruit, peeled, thinly sliced

2 tablespoons orange marmalade

1 Heat oven to 450°F. Bake pie crust as directed on box for One-Crust Baked Shell, using 9-inch tart pan with removable bottom or 9-inch glass pie plate. Cool completely on cooling rack, about 15 minutes.

2 In medium bowl, mix filling ingredients with whisk until well blended. Pour into cooled baked crust. Arrange strawberries and kiwifruit on filling.

3 In small microwavable bowl, microwave 2 tablespoons marmalade on High 5 to 10 seconds or until melted. Brush over fruit. Refrigerate about 1 hour or until set before serving. To remove tart from sides of pan, place the pan on a wide, short can and pull down the side of the pan (see page 80). If necessary, use a thin-bladed knife to loosen crust from the side of the pan. Cover and refrigerate any remaining tart.

High Altitude (3500–6500 ft): No change.

1 Serving: Calories 290; Total Fat 11g (Saturated Fat 5g; Trans Fat 0g); Cholesterol 15mg; Sodium 330mg; Total Carbohydrate 43g (Dietary Fiber 1g) **Exchanges:** 1 Starch, 2 Other Carbohydrate, 2 Fat **Carbohydrate Choices:** 3

Pie Tip Sometimes, pie crust bubbles up when it's baked. If bubbles form, press them down gently with the back of a wooden spoon. Continue baking until the crust is done.

savory pies and quiches

Classic Chicken Pot Pie, page 160

classic chicken pot pie

Prep Time: 25 Minutes ✳ Start to Finish: 1 Hour 25 Minutes ✳ 6 servings

CRUST

1 box (15 oz) Pillsbury refrigerated pie crusts, softened as directed on box

FILLING

⅓ cup butter or margarine

⅓ cup chopped onion *celery*

⅓ cup all-purpose flour *3 Tbsp Better Batter*

½ teaspoon salt

¼ teaspoon pepper

1 can (14 oz) chicken broth

½ cup milk *whole + non-fat*

2½ cups shredded cooked chicken or turkey

2 cups frozen mixed vegetables, thawed

1 Heat oven to 425°F. Make pie crusts as directed on box for Two-Crust Pie, using 9-inch glass pie plate.

2 In 2-quart saucepan, melt butter over medium heat. Add onion; cook and stir about 2 minutes or until tender. Stir in flour, salt and pepper until well blended. Cook 2 to 3 minutes, stirring constantly. Gradually stir in broth and milk, cooking and stirring until bubbly and thickened. Stir in chicken and thawed mixed vegetables. Remove from heat. Spoon chicken mixture into crust-lined pie plate.

3 Cut second crust into strips. Place 5 to 7 strips across filling. Place cross-strips over tops of first strips (see photo on page 159). Seal edge and flute. Cover crust edge with foil to prevent excessive browning; remove foil during last 15 minutes of baking.

4 Bake 30 to 40 minutes or until crust is golden brown. Let stand 15 to 20 minutes before serving.

High Altitude (3500–6500 ft): No change.

1 Serving: Calories 600; Total Fat 34g (Saturated Fat 13g; Trans Fat 1g); Cholesterol 90mg; Sodium 940mg; Total Carbohydrate 50g (Dietary Fiber 4g) **Exchanges:** 3½ Starch, 2 Lean Meat, 5 Fat **Carbohydrate Choices:** 3

Pie Tip Other frozen thawed vegetables can be used for the mixed vegetables. Try 2 cups of frozen, thawed, peas, corn or green beans.

See photo on page 159.

chicken divan pot pie

Prep Time: 30 Minutes ✳ Start to Finish: 1 Hour 5 Minutes ✳ 6 servings

CRUST

1 box (15 oz) Pillsbury refrigerated pie crusts, softened as directed on package

FILLING

3 tablespoons butter or margarine

3 tablespoons all-purpose flour

¼ teaspoon pepper

½ cup chicken broth

¼ cup milk

1 cup shredded American cheese (4 oz)

2 cups diced cooked chicken or turkey

1 box (9 oz) frozen cut broccoli, thawed, well drained

1 Heat oven to 425°F. Make pie crusts as directed on box for Two-Crust Pie, using 9-inch glass pie plate.

2 In 2-quart saucepan, melt butter over medium-low heat. Stir in flour and pepper; cook until mixture is smooth and bubbly. Gradually add broth and milk, stirring constantly, until mixture boils and thickens.

3 Add cheese; stir until melted. Stir in chicken and broccoli. Pour mixture into crust-lined pie plate. Top with second crust; seal edge and flute. Cut slits in several places in top crust.

4 Bake 30 to 35 minutes or until crust is golden brown and filling is bubbly. Cover crust edge with strips of foil after first 15 to 20 minutes of baking to prevent excessive browning. Cool 10 minutes before serving.

High Altitude (3500–6500 ft): No change.

1 Serving: Calories 550; Total Fat 34g (Saturated Fat 15g; Trans Fat 0g); Cholesterol 85mg; Sodium 750mg; Total Carbohydrate 41g (Dietary Fiber 1g) **Exchanges:** 1½ Starch, 1 Other Carbohydrate, 2 Lean Meat, 5½ Fat **Carbohydrate Choices:** 3

Pie Tip If you have other cheese on hand, such as a mild Cheddar, Colby or Swiss cheese, shred it and use it instead of the American cheese.

rustic chicken club

Sharon Kube | West Lafayette, IN | Bake-Off® Contest 41, 2004

Prep Time: 40 Minutes ✳ Start to Finish: 1 Hour 10 Minutes ✳ 6 servings

CRUST

1 Pillsbury refrigerated pie crust (from 15-oz box), softened as directed on box

FILLING

4 tablespoons mayonnaise

¾ cup shredded Monterey Jack cheese (3 oz)

2 cups chopped cooked chicken or turkey breast

1 tablespoon Dijon mustard

1 tablespoon fresh lemon juice

½ to 1 teaspoon freshly ground black pepper

¼ teaspoon celery salt

Dash salt

Dash ground red pepper (cayenne)

6 slices bacon, crisply cooked and crumbled

¾ cup shredded Cheddar cheese (3 oz)

1 egg yolk

1 tablespoon water

1 tablespoon sesame seed

TOPPINGS

1 cup chopped romaine lettuce

1 medium tomato, seeded, finely chopped

¼ cup chopped green onions (4 medium)

1 Heat oven to 400°F. Line cookie sheet with heavy-duty foil. Unroll pie crust; place crust flat between 2 sheets of waxed paper. With rolling pin, roll crust into 14×12-inch oval. Remove top waxed paper; carefully turn pie crust over onto cookie sheet. Remove waxed paper.

2 Spread 2 tablespoons of the mayonnaise evenly over crust to within 2 inches of edge. Sprinkle Monterey Jack cheese over mayonnaise.

3 In small bowl, mix chicken, remaining 2 tablespoons mayonnaise, the mustard, lemon juice, black pepper, celery salt, salt and ground red pepper. Spoon mixture over Monterey Jack cheese. Sprinkle with crumbled bacon. Sprinkle Cheddar cheese over top.

4 Fold 2-inch edge of crust up over filling, pleating crust as necessary and leaving 5×7-inch oval opening in center. Gently press down on edge to securely enclose filling.

5 In small bowl, beat egg yolk and water with fork. Generously brush yolk mixture over crust; sprinkle crust with sesame seed.

6 Bake 20 to 25 minutes or until crust is golden brown. Cool 10 minutes. With metal spatula, gently lift edge; slide onto serving plate. Sprinkle lettuce over filling; press down lightly. Top with tomato and onions. Cut into 6 wedges to serve.

High Altitude (3500–6500 ft): No change.

1 Serving: Calories 630; Total Fat 42g (Saturated Fat 16g; Trans Fat 0g); Cholesterol 120mg; Sodium 860mg; Total Carbohydrate 37g (Dietary Fiber 0g) **Exchanges:** 1 Starch, 1½ Other Carbohydrate, 3½ Medium-Fat Meat, 4½ Fat **Carbohydrate Choices:** 2½

super easy chicken pot pie

Prep Time: 15 Minutes * Start to Finish: 55 Minutes * 6 servings

CRUST

1 box (15 oz) Pillsbury refrigerated pie crusts, softened as directed on box

FILLING

1 can (18.6 oz) ready-to-serve chicken pot pie style soup

2 cups frozen mixed vegetables, thawed, drained

2 tablespoons all-purpose flour

1 Heat oven to 425°F. Make pie crusts as directed on box for Two-Crust Pie, using 9-inch glass pie plate.

2 In 2-quart saucepan, heat soup, thawed vegetables and flour until warm. Spoon into crust-lined pie plate. Top with second crust; seal edge and flute. Cut slits in several places in top crust.

3 Bake 30 to 35 minutes or until crust is golden brown. After 15 minutes of baking, cover crust edge with foil to prevent excessive browning. Let stand 5 minutes before serving. Cut into wedges.

High Altitude (3500–6500 ft): No change.

1 Serving: Calories 390; Total Fat 20g (Saturated Fat 7g; Trans Fat 0g); Cholesterol 15mg; Sodium 620mg; Total Carbohydrate 47g (Dietary Fiber 1g) **Exchanges:** 1 Starch, 2½ Other Carbohydrate, 3½ Fat **Carbohydrate Choices:** 3

Pie Tip To quickly thaw the frozen mixed vegetables, place them in a strainer and rinse with warm water until thawed. Drain well.

fiesta chicken empanada

Janielle Fisher | Newark, DE | Bake-Off® Contest 39, 2000

Prep Time: 15 Minutes ✲ Start to Finish: 40 Minutes ✲ 6 servings

CRUST

1 box (15 oz) Pillsbury refrigerated pie crusts, softened as directed on box

FILLING

1 tablespoon olive oil

1 medium onion, sliced

½ medium red bell pepper, cut into 2×¼-inch strips

½ medium green bell pepper, cut into 2×¼-inch strips

½ medium yellow bell pepper, cut into 2×¼-inch strips

1 can (10 oz) chunk white chicken breast in water, drained

4 teaspoons dried fajita seasoning

½ cup cheese 'n salsa dip (from 15-oz jar)

1 egg, beaten

TOPPINGS

Sour cream, if desired

Additional cheese 'n salsa dip, if desired

1 Heat oven to 425°F. On ungreased 14-inch pizza pan or cookie sheet, unroll 1 pie crust.

2 In 10-inch skillet, heat oil over medium-high heat. Add onion and bell peppers; cook 5 minutes, stirring occasionally, until tender. Stir in chicken and fajita seasoning.

3 Spoon chicken mixture evenly onto crust in pan to within 1 inch of edge. Spread ½ cup dip over chicken mixture. Brush edge of crust with water. Remove second crust from pouch. Unroll crust; place over filling, pressing edge firmly to seal. Brush top with beaten egg.

4 Bake 20 to 25 minutes or until deep golden brown, covering crust edge with foil after 10 to 15 minutes of baking to prevent excessive browning. Cut into wedges; serve with sour cream and dip.

High Altitude (3500–6500 ft): In step 4, bake 25 to 30 minutes.

1 Serving: Calories 420; Total Fat 24g (Saturated Fat 8g; Trans Fat 0g); Cholesterol 65mg; Sodium 1000mg; Total Carbohydrate 41g (Dietary Fiber 1g) **Exchanges:** 2½ Starch, ½ Vegetable, 4½ Fat **Carbohydrate Choices:** 3

 You can use 1½ bell peppers of the same color if you prefer not to purchase 3 different colored peppers. The flavor may change slightly because red and yellow peppers are milder than green peppers.

chicken-asiago-spinach quiche

Will Sperry | Bunker Hill, WV | Bake-Off® Contest 43, 2008

Prep Time: 30 Minutes ✳ Start to Finish: 1 Hour 25 Minutes ✳ 8 servings

CRUST

1 Pillsbury refrigerated pie crust (from 15-oz box), softened as directed on box

FILLING

2 tablespoons vegetable oil

½ teaspoon finely chopped garlic

1 medium onion, chopped (½ cup)

½ cup cooked real bacon pieces (from 2.5-oz package)

1 cup chopped cooked chicken or turkey

1 box (9 oz) frozen spinach, thawed, squeezed to drain and chopped

1 container (8 oz) sour cream

¼ teaspoon salt

¼ teaspoon garlic powder

⅛ teaspoon pepper

2 cups shredded sharp Cheddar cheese (8 oz)

1½ cups shredded Asiago cheese (6 oz)

3 eggs

½ cup whipping cream

1 Heat oven to 375°F. Unroll pie crust in 9-inch regular or 9½-inch deep-dish glass pie plate; press firmly against bottom and side. Flute edge as desired. Prick bottom of crust several times with fork. Bake 10 minutes. Cool completely on cooling rack, about 15 minutes.

2 Meanwhile, in 10-inch skillet, heat oil over medium heat until hot. Add garlic and onion; cook 2 to 3 minutes, stirring occasionally, until onion is tender. Reduce heat to low. Stir in bacon, chicken and spinach; toss to combine. Remove from heat; transfer mixture to large bowl.

3 Stir sour cream, salt, garlic powder and pepper into spinach mixture until well blended. Stir in cheeses.

4 In small bowl, beat eggs and whipping cream with fork or whisk until well blended. Gently fold into spinach mixture until well blended. Pour filling into pie crust.

5 Bake 15 minutes. Cover crust edge with foil to prevent excessive browning. Bake 20 to 25 minutes longer or until center is set and edge of crust is golden brown. Let stand 15 minutes before serving.

High Altitude (3500–6500 ft): No change.

1 Serving: Calories 550; Total Fat 42g (Saturated Fat 21g; Trans Fat 0.5g); Cholesterol 185mg; Sodium 760mg; Total Carbohydrate 18g (Dietary Fiber 2g) **Exchanges:** 1 Starch, 3 Medium-Fat Meat, 5½ Fat **Carbohydrate Choices:** 1

chicken enchilada quiche

Jessica Barton | Eugene, OR | Bake-Off® Contest 41, 2004

Prep Time: 15 Minutes ✳ Start to Finish: 1 Hour 30 Minutes ✳ 8 servings

CRUST

1 Pillsbury refrigerated pie crust (from 15-oz box), softened as directed on box

FILLING

4 eggs

1 cup half-and-half or milk

1 can (12.5 oz) chunk chicken breast in water, drained (1½ cups)

1½ cups broken tortilla chips

2 cups shredded Monterey Jack cheese (8 oz)

1 cup shredded Cheddar cheese (4 oz)

1 cup chunky-style salsa

1 can (4.5 oz) chopped green chiles

½ teaspoon salt

Pepper to taste, if desired

SERVE WITH, IF DESIRED

Sour cream

Additional salsa

1 Heat oven to 350°F. Place pie crust in 9- or 9½-inch glass deep-dish pie plate as directed on box for One-Crust Filled Pie.

2 In medium bowl, beat eggs with whisk until blended. Beat in half-and-half. Stir in chicken, chips, both cheeses, 1 cup salsa, the green chiles and salt. Pour into crust-lined pie plate. Sprinkle pepper over filling.

3 Bake 55 to 65 minutes or until crust is light golden brown and knife inserted in center comes out clean. Let stand 10 minutes before serving. Cut into wedges. Serve with sour cream and additional salsa.

High Altitude (3500–6500 ft): Heat oven to 375°F. After 15 minutes of baking, cover crust edge with foil to prevent excessive browning.

1 Serving: Calories 590; Total Fat 38g (Saturated Fat 17g; Trans Fat 0g); Cholesterol 185mg; Sodium 1110mg; Total Carbohydrate 41g (Dietary Fiber 1g) **Exchanges:** 1 Starch, 2 Other Carbohydrate, 1 Medium-Fat Meat, 2 High-Fat Meat, 2½ Fat **Carbohydrate Choices:** 3

chicken caesar club salad pie

Prep Time: 20 Minutes ✳ Start to Finish: 55 Minutes ✳ 4 servings

CRUST
1 Pillsbury refrigerated pie crust (from 15-oz box), softened as directed on box

FILLING
2 packages (6 oz each) refrigerated cooked chicken breast strips

½ cup Caesar dressing

2 tablespoons cooked real bacon pieces (from 2.8-oz package)

2 tablespoons shredded Parmesan cheese (½ oz)

TOPPING
2 cups sliced romaine lettuce

½ cup halved grape or cherry tomatoes

1 Heat oven to 400°F. On ungreased large cookie sheet, unroll pie crust. Roll or press into 12-inch round.

2 Arrange chicken on crust to within 1½ inches of edge. Drizzle 2 tablespoons of the dressing over chicken; sprinkle with bacon. Carefully fold 1½-inch edge of crust over chicken, pleating crust slightly as necessary. Sprinkle 2 teaspoons of the cheese over crust edge.

3 Bake 20 to 25 minutes or until crust is golden brown. Cool on cookie sheet 10 minutes. With metal spatula, gently lift edge; slide pie onto serving plate. Sprinkle with lettuce and tomatoes. Drizzle with remaining dressing. Sprinkle with remaining cheese. Cut into wedges to serve.

High Altitude (3500–6500 ft): No change.

1 Serving: Calories 550; Total Fat 36g (Saturated Fat 9g; Trans Fat 0g); Cholesterol 75mg; Sodium 1210mg; Total Carbohydrate 30g (Dietary Fiber 1g) **Exchanges:** 2 Starch, 3 High-Fat Meat, 2 Fat **Carbohydrate Choices:** 2

Pie Tip This is a great recipe to finish up that leftover cooked chicken. Two cups of coarsely chopped or shredded rotisserie or cooked chicken can be used in place of the chicken breast strips.

chicken taco wedges

Prep Time: 10 Minutes ✳ Start to Finish: 30 Minutes ✳ 6 servings

CRUST

1 box (15 oz) Pillsbury refrigerated pie crusts, softened as directed on box

FILLING

¼ cup mayonnaise or salad dressing

¼ cup chunky-style salsa

1 cup cubed cooked chicken or turkey

1 cup chopped tomato (1 large)

¼ cup sliced green onions (4 medium)

1 cup shredded Cheddar cheese (4 oz)

TOPPINGS, IF DESIRED

Shredded lettuce

Sliced ripe olives

Sour cream

Additional salsa

1 Heat oven to 450°F. On ungreased large cookie sheet, unroll crusts.

2 In small bowl, mix mayonnaise and ¼ cup salsa. Spread mixture evenly over each crust. Sprinkle half of each crust with ½ cup chicken, ½ cup tomato, 2 tablespoons onions and ½ cup cheese. Fold untopped half of each crust over filling; do not seal.

3 Bake 14 to 18 minutes or until golden brown. Cut into wedges. Top with lettuce, ripe olives and sour cream. Serve with additional salsa.

High Altitude (3500–6500 ft): No change.

1 Serving: Calories 500; Total Fat 34g (Saturated Fat 12g; Trans Fat 0g); Cholesterol 55mg; Sodium 550mg; Total Carbohydrate 37g (Dietary Fiber 0g) **Exchanges:** 2½ Starch, 1 Medium-Fat Meat, 5 Fat **Carbohydrate Choices:** 2½

chicken and vegetables with pastry wedges

Prep Time: 35 Minutes * Start to Finish: 45 Minutes * 6 servings

PASTRY WEDGES

1 Pillsbury refrigerated pie crust (from 15-oz box), softened as directed on box

1 teaspoon grated Parmesan cheese

½ teaspoon dried thyme leaves

FILLING

3 teaspoons olive oil

2 cups sliced baby portabella mushrooms (about 6 oz)

1 tablespoon butter or margarine

6 boneless skinless chicken breasts (about 2 lbs), quartered

1 cup ready-to-eat baby-cut carrots, quartered lengthwise

1 teaspoon salt

¼ teaspoon pepper

1 cup frozen small whole onions (from 1-lb bag)

½ cup white wine or chicken broth

3 tablespoons all-purpose flour

2 tablespoons water

½ cup whipping cream

½ cup frozen sweet peas (from 1-lb bag)

1 Heat oven to 450°F. On ungreased cookie sheet, unroll pie crust. Sprinkle evenly with cheese and thyme; roll in lightly with rolling pin. Prick crust generously with fork. With pastry wheel or sharp knife, cut into 12 wedges; separate slightly. Bake 7 to 10 minutes or until light golden brown.

2 Meanwhile, in 12-inch skillet, heat 2 teaspoons of the oil over medium-high heat until hot. Add mushrooms; cook 2 to 3 minutes, stirring frequently, until tender. Remove mushrooms from skillet; place in bowl. Set aside.

3 In same skillet, melt butter and remaining 1 teaspoon oil over medium-high heat. Add chicken and carrots; sprinkle with salt and pepper. Cook 5 to 7 minutes, stirring occasionally, until browned. Stir in onions and wine. Heat to boiling. Reduce heat to medium-low. Cover; cook about 20 minutes or until chicken is no longer pink in center.

4 In small bowl, mix flour and water until smooth. Add to juices in skillet; cook over medium heat, stirring constantly, until bubbly and thickened. Stir in whipping cream, peas and cooked mushrooms. Cook 3 to 4 minutes, stirring frequently, until hot. Serve chicken mixture with pastry wedges.

High Altitude (3500–6500 ft): In step 3, add ¼ cup water with the wine. Thaw peas before using in step 4.

1 Serving: Calories 640; Total Fat 34g (Saturated Fat 14g; Trans Fat 0g); Cholesterol 130mg; Sodium 910mg; Total Carbohydrate 47g (Dietary Fiber 2g) **Exchanges:** 3 Starch, 4 Lean Meat, 4 Fat **Carbohydrate Choices:** 3

 Pie Tip Portabella mushrooms are a firmer mushroom and add texture to this creamy dish. You can use 2 cups of your favorite sliced mushrooms if you like. Shiitake or crimini add a little more flavor than the popular white button mushrooms.

deep-dish turkey pie

Prep Time: 20 Minutes ✳ Start to Finish: 1 Hour 20 Minutes ✳ 6 servings

FILLING

2 tablespoons butter or margarine

¼ cup chopped celery

¼ cup chopped onion (½ medium)

1 can (10¾ oz) condensed cream of chicken soup

1 cup milk

½ teaspoon poultry seasoning

¼ teaspoon salt

¼ teaspoon pepper

4 cups cubed cooked turkey or chicken

1 bag (14 oz) frozen broccoli florets, thawed, drained

CRUST

1 Pillsbury refrigerated pie crust (from 15-oz box), softened as directed on box

1 Heat oven to 400°F. In 3-quart saucepan or Dutch oven, melt butter over medium heat. Add celery and onion; cook and stir until tender. Stir in soup, milk, poultry seasoning, salt and pepper. Cook until hot.

2 Gently stir in turkey and thawed broccoli. Pour into ungreased 10-inch quiche dish or 2-quart casserole.

3 Unroll pie crust. Place crust over turkey mixture. Roll up edge of crust to fit top of quiche dish; flute edge. Cut slits in several places in top crust.

4 Bake 40 to 50 minutes or until golden brown. Let stand 10 minutes before serving.

High Altitude (3500–6500 ft): No change.

1 Serving: Calories 600; Total Fat 33g (Saturated Fat 12g; Trans Fat 0g); Cholesterol 105mg; Sodium 890mg; Total Carbohydrate 45g (Dietary Fiber 2g) **Exchanges:** 1½ Starch, 1 Other Carbohydrate, 1 Vegetable, 3½ Lean Meat, 4½ Fat **Carbohydrate Choices:** 3

Pie Tip Forgot to put the broccoli in the refrigerator last night to thaw? You can quickly thaw the frozen broccoli by placing it in a colander or strainer and rinsing with warm water until thawed. Drain well.

patchwork turkey pot pie

Prep Time: 15 Minutes ✳ Start to Finish: 1 Hour 35 Minutes ✳ 6 servings

FILLING

2 cups diced (¼ to ½ inch) cooked turkey breast

2 cups refrigerated cooked diced potatoes with onions (from 20-oz bag)

2 cups frozen mixed vegetables

1 jar (4.5 oz) sliced mushrooms, drained

½ cup sour cream

1 jar (12 oz) turkey gravy

¼ teaspoon dried sage leaves

CRUST

1 Pillsbury refrigerated pie crust (from 15-oz box), softened as directed on box

1 Heat oven to 375°F. Spray 3-quart casserole with cooking spray. In large bowl, mix turkey, potatoes, frozen vegetables, mushrooms, sour cream, gravy and sage; spoon mixture into casserole.

2 Unroll pie crust on work surface. Cut into 1½-inch-wide strips, then cut in opposite direction, making 1½-inch square pieces (not all will be perfectly square). Starting with rounded-edge pieces around edge of casserole, arrange pie crust pieces over top of mixture, overlapping each piece (see photo).

3 Bake 1 hour 15 minutes to 1 hour 20 minutes or until crust is golden brown and edges are bubbly.

High Altitude (3500–6500 ft): Thaw frozen vegetables before adding to casserole.

1 Serving: Calories 390; Total Fat 18g (Saturated Fat 7g; Trans Fat 0g); Cholesterol 60mg; Sodium 760mg; Total Carbohydrate 40g (Dietary Fiber 4g) **Exchanges:** 2 Starch, ½ Other Carbohydrate, 1 Vegetable, 1½ Very Lean Meat, 3 Fat **Carbohydrate Choices:** 2½

patchwork chicken pot pie: Substitute 2 cups diced rotisserie or cooked chicken for the turkey and a 12-oz jar of chicken gravy for the turkey gravy.

Making Patchwork Crust

Cover top of turkey mixture with pie crust squares, overlapping each square slightly.

spinach, sausage and feta quiche

Kathleen Haller | Baltimore, MD | Bake-Off® Contest 43, 2008

Prep Time: 30 Minutes ✳ Start to Finish: 1 Hour 30 Minutes ✳ 8 servings

CRUST

1 Pillsbury refrigerated pie crust (from 15-oz box), softened as directed on box

FILLING

½ cup finely crushed garlic and butter croutons

1 cup shredded Cheddar cheese (4 oz)

4 oz smoked turkey sausage, sliced

1 box (9 oz) frozen spinach, thawed, squeezed to drain and chopped

2 tablespoons finely chopped onion

1 cup crumbled feta cheese (4 oz)

4 eggs

1½ cups half-and-half

¼ teaspoon salt, if desired

⅛ teaspoon pepper

8 cherry tomatoes, cut into quarters

1 Heat oven to 350°F. Place pie crust in 9-inch glass pie plate or quiche dish as directed on box for One-Crust Filled Pie.

2 Cover bottom of pie crust with crushed croutons; sprinkle with Cheddar cheese. Layer sausage slices on cheese; top with spinach, onion and feta cheese.

3 In large bowl, beat eggs, half-and-half, salt and pepper with whisk until well blended; slowly pour into pie crust.

4 Bake 45 minutes. Cover crust edge with foil to prevent excessive browning. Bake 5 to 15 minutes longer or until knife inserted in center comes out clean. Let stand 15 minutes before serving. Top with tomatoes.

High Altitude (3500–6500 ft): No change.

1 Serving: Calories 350; Total Fat 24g (Saturated Fat 12g; Trans Fat 0.5g); Cholesterol 145mg; Sodium 600mg; Total Carbohydrate 19g (Dietary Fiber 1g) **Exchanges:** ½ Starch, 1 Other Carbohydrate, 1½ Medium-Fat Meat, 3 Fat **Carbohydrate Choices:** 1

ground beef pot pie

Prep Time: 20 Minutes ✳ Start to Finish: 1 Hour 5 Minutes ✳ 6 servings

CRUST

1 box (15 oz) Pillsbury refrigerated pie crusts, softened as directed on box

FILLING

1 lb lean (at least 80%) ground beef

1 medium onion, chopped (½ cup)

1 teaspoon garlic salt

½ teaspoon pepper

3 tablespoons cornstarch

3 cups frozen southern-style diced hash brown potatoes (from 32-oz bag), thawed

3 medium carrots, sliced (1½ cups)

1 jar (12 oz) beef gravy

1 Heat oven to 450°F. Make pie crusts as directed on box for Two-Crust Pie, using 9-inch glass pie plate.

2 In 12-inch skillet, cook beef, onion, garlic salt and pepper over medium-high heat 5 to 7 minutes, stirring frequently, until beef is thoroughly cooked; drain.

3 Stir cornstarch into beef mixture until well mixed. Stir in potatoes, carrots and gravy. Cook 5 to 6 minutes over medium-high heat, stirring constantly, until mixture is hot. Spoon mixture into crust-lined pie plate. Top with second crust; seal edge and flute. Cut slits in several places in top crust. Cover crust edge with foil to prevent excessive browning.

4 Bake 35 to 40 minutes or until crust is golden brown. Cool 5 minutes before serving.

High Altitude (3500–6500 ft): No change.

1 Serving: Calories 590; Total Fat 29g (Saturated Fat 11g; Trans Fat 0.5g); Cholesterol 60mg; Sodium 850mg; Total Carbohydrate 66g (Dietary Fiber 3g) **Exchanges:** 3 Starch, 1½ Other Carbohydrate, 1 Medium-Fat Meat, 4 Fat **Carbohydrate Choices:** 4½

jack-o'-lantern sloppy joe pie

Prep Time: 50 Minutes * Start to Finish: 50 Minutes * 4 servings

CRUST

1 Pillsbury refrigerated pie crust (from 15-oz box), softened as directed on box

1 egg yolk, if desired

1 teaspoon water, if desired

Red and yellow food color, if desired

FILLING

1½ lb bulk seasoned turkey sausage

1 medium onion, chopped (½ cup)

1 cup chunky-style salsa

½ cup chili sauce

2 tablespoons packed brown sugar

1 cup frozen whole kernel corn

1 can (4.5 oz) chopped green chiles, undrained

2 tablespoons chopped fresh cilantro, if desired

1 Heat oven to 450°F. On ungreased cookie sheet, unroll pie crust. With sharp knife, cut jack-o'-lantern face from crust. If desired, use cutout pieces to decorate jack-o'-lantern; secure each with small amount of water. Prick crust with fork. In small bowl, mix egg yolk, 1 teaspoon water and the food color; brush on crust. Bake 9 to 11 minutes or until crust is light golden brown.

2 Meanwhile, in 12-inch nonstick skillet, crumble sausage. Add onion; cook 8 to 10 minutes, stirring occasionally, until sausage is no longer pink. Stir in all remaining ingredients except cilantro. Heat to boiling. Reduce heat to medium-low; simmer 8 to 10 minutes, stirring occasionally, until corn is cooked and sauce is of desired consistency.

3 Stir cilantro into sausage mixture. Carefully place warm baked pie crust on sausage mixture.

High Altitude (3500–6500 ft): No change.

1 Serving: Calories 690; Total Fat 32g (Saturated Fat 9g; Trans Fat 0.5g); Cholesterol 165mg; Sodium 2,750mg; Total Carbohydrate 56g (Dietary Fiber 4g) **Exchanges:** 2½ Starch, 1 Other Carbohydrate, 5 Medium-Fat Meat, 1 Fat **Carbohydrate Choices:** 4

Pie Tip Enjoy this kid-friendly skillet pie any time of the year without the cute jack-o'-lantern face. Be sure to prick the crust generously with a fork before baking so the crust stays flat. If you like a spicier pie, use 1½ lb bulk Italian sausage instead of the turkey sausage.

deep-dish ground beef pot pies

Prep Time: 25 Minutes ✳ Start to Finish: 1 Hour ✳ 4 servings

FILLING

1 lb lean (at least 80%) ground beef

½ cup chopped onion (1 medium)

2 cups diced (½ inch) unpeeled russet potatoes

2 cups frozen mixed vegetables

1 can (14.5 oz) diced tomatoes with basil, garlic and oregano, undrained

1 jar (12 oz) beef gravy

⅛ teaspoon pepper

CRUST

1 Pillsbury refrigerated pie crust (from 15-oz box), softened as directed on box

1 egg white, beaten

1 to 2 tablespoons finely chopped fresh parsley

1 Heat oven to 425°F. Spray 4 (2-cup) individual ovenproof bowls with cooking spray; place bowls in 15×10×1-inch pan. In 12-inch nonstick skillet or 4-quart Dutch oven, cook beef and onion over medium-high heat, stirring frequently, until beef is thoroughly cooked; drain.

2 Stir in potatoes, frozen vegetables, tomatoes, gravy and pepper. Reduce heat to medium-low; cover and cook 8 to 10 minutes, stirring occasionally, until potatoes are almost tender.

3 Meanwhile, unroll pie crust on work surface. With 5-inch round cutter, cut 4 rounds from crust.

4 Spoon beef mixture evenly into bowls. Place crusts over beef mixture; seal to edges of bowls. Cut slits in several places in each crust. Brush crusts with egg white; sprinkle with parsley.

5 Bake 30 to 35 minutes or until crusts are golden brown.

High Altitude (3500–6500 ft): In step 2, reduce heat to medium; cover and cook 10 to 15 minutes.

1 Serving: Calories 490; Total Fat 23g (Saturated Fat 9g; Trans Fat 1g); Cholesterol 75mg; Sodium 1100mg; Total Carbohydrate 43g (Dietary Fiber 4g) **Exchanges:** 1½ Starch, 1 Other Carbohydrate, 1 Vegetable, 3 Medium-Fat Meat, 1½ Fat **Carbohydrate Choices:** 3

 To make one large pot pie, spoon beef mixture into sprayed or greased 2-quart casserole. Cover mixture with uncut pie crust; seal edge against inside of casserole. Continue as directed above; bake at 425°F 30 to 35 minutes or until crust is golden brown.

california cheeseburger pie

Prep Time: 25 Minutes * Start to Finish: 1 Hour 15 Minutes * 8 servings

CRUST
1 box (15 oz) Pillsbury
   refrigerated pie crusts,
   softened as directed on box

FILLING
1½ lb lean (at least 80%)
   ground beef

1 large onion, chopped (1 cup)

2 cups cubed prepared cheese
   product (from 16-oz loaf)

½ cup Thousand Island
   dressing

2 teaspoons yellow mustard

16 round dill pickle chips or
   8 oblong dill pickle slices

¼ teaspoon sesame seed

TOPPINGS
Lettuce leaves

2 plum (Roma) tomatoes,
   sliced

1 Heat oven to 375°F. Make pie crusts as directed on box for Two-Crust Pie, using 9-inch glass pie plate.

2 In 12-inch skillet, cook beef and onion over medium-high heat, stirring frequently, until beef is thoroughly cooked; drain.

3 Stir in cheese, dressing and mustard. Reduce heat to low; cook 2 to 3 minutes, stirring occasionally, until cheese is melted. Spoon beef mixture into crust-lined pie plate. Arrange pickle chips over beef mixture.

4 Top with second crust; seal edge and flute. Sprinkle with sesame seed. Cut slits in several places in top crust. Cover crust edge with foil to prevent excessive browning; remove foil during last 15 minutes of baking.

5 Bake 30 to 40 minutes or until crust is golden brown. Let stand 10 minutes before serving. Top pie with lettuce and tomatoes. Serve with ketchup and mustard, if desired.

High Altitude (3500–6500 ft): No change.

1 Serving: Calories 600; Total Fat 41g (Saturated Fat 16g; Trans Fat 1g); Cholesterol 100mg; Sodium 1330mg; Total Carbohydrate 35g (Dietary Fiber 0g) **Exchanges:** 1½ Starch, 1 Other Carbohydrate, 2½ High-Fat Meat, 4 Fat **Carbohydrate Choices:** 2

 Pie Tip Prepared cheese product is the cheese in the yellow box. You can find it on the shelf near the dairy area in the supermarket. Want to add a little kick to your cheeseburger pie? Use the Mexican cheese product with jalapeño peppers.

tex-mex meatball pie

Prep Time: 10 Minutes ✳ Start to Finish: 55 Minutes ✳ 6 servings

CRUST

1 Pillsbury refrigerated pie crust (from 15-oz box), softened as directed on box

FILLING

18 frozen cooked meatballs (about 1 inch), thawed

1 cup frozen whole kernel corn

½ cup chunky-style salsa

¾ cup shredded Cheddar cheese (3 oz)

TOPPINGS

1 cup shredded lettuce

¼ cup sour cream

Additional chunky-style salsa or chopped tomatoes

1 Heat oven to 375°F. On ungreased cookie sheet, unroll pie crust. Place meatballs on center of crust.

2 In small bowl, mix corn and ½ cup salsa. Spoon corn mixture over meatballs. Carefully fold 2-inch edge of crust over filling, pleating crust slightly as necessary (see photo).

3 Bake 35 to 40 minutes or until crust is deep golden brown. Sprinkle with cheese. Bake 3 to 5 minutes longer or until cheese is melted.

4 Serve with lettuce, sour cream and additional salsa. Serve immediately.

High Altitude (3500–6500 ft): No change.

1 Serving: Calories 340; Total Fat 20g (Saturated Fat 9g; Trans Fat 0g); Cholesterol 60mg; Sodium 640mg; Total Carbohydrate 29g (Dietary Fiber 0g) **Exchanges:** 1½ Starch, ½ Other Carbohydrate, 1 High-Fat Meat, 2 Fat **Carbohydrate Choices:** 2

Pie Tip If the meatballs are larger than 1 inch, cut them in half before placing on the pie crust. Taco-flavored Cheddar cheese is also great in this fun dinner pie.

Shaping Meatball Pie Crust

Carefully fold edge of crust over filling, pleating crust slightly as necessary.

savory beef and mushroom pie

Prep Time: 35 Minutes ❋ Start to Finish: 1 Hour 20 Minutes ❋ 6 servings

CRUST

1 box (15 oz) Pillsbury refrigerated pie crusts, softened as directed on box

FILLING

1 lb lean (at least 80%) ground beef

1½ cups sliced fresh mushrooms

¾ cup chopped onions

3 tablespoons all-purpose flour

1 package savory herb with garlic soup mix (from 2.4-oz box)

½ cup half-and-half

1 package (3 oz) cream cheese, softened

½ cup shredded Swiss cheese (2 oz)

1 Make pie crusts as directed on box for Two-Crust Pie, using 9-inch glass pie plate.

2 Heat oven to 375°F. In 12-inch nonstick skillet, cook beef, mushrooms, onions and flour over medium heat 10 to 12 minutes, stirring frequently, until beef is thoroughly cooked and liquid from mushrooms has evaporated.

3 Stir in soup mix and half-and-half. Add cream cheese; cook until cream cheese has melted and mixture is hot, stirring constantly. Remove from heat. Stir in Swiss cheese.

4 Pour beef mixture into crust-lined pan. Top with second crust; seal edge and flute. Cut slits in several places in top crust.

5 Bake 35 to 45 minutes or until crust is golden brown. Let stand 10 minutes before serving. Cut into wedges to serve.

High Altitude (3500–6500 ft): Cook beef mixture over medium-high heat. After baking pie 20 minutes, cover crust edge with strips of foil to prevent excessive browning.

1 Serving: Calories 610; Total Fat 37g (Saturated Fat 16g; Trans Fat 1g); Cholesterol 85mg; Sodium 1380mg; Total Carbohydrate 49g (Dietary Fiber 1g) **Exchanges:** 1½ Starch, 2 Other Carbohydrate, 2 Medium-Fat Meat, 4½ Fat **Carbohydrate Choices:** 3

Pie Tip To ensure the pie crust bakes completely through, assemble this pie with very hot filling. Heat from the filling cooks the crust from the inside while the oven heat bakes it from the outside.

beef empanadas

Prep Time: 20 Minutes ✳ Start to Finish: 45 Minutes ✳ 6 servings

1 lb lean (at least 80%) ground beef

1 medium onion, chopped (½ cup)

½ teaspoon chili powder

¼ teaspoon salt

1 can (14.5 oz) diced tomatoes with mild green chiles, well drained

1 box (15 oz) Pillsbury refrigerated pie crusts, softened as directed on box

½ cup shredded Monterey Jack cheese (2 oz)

1 egg, beaten

1 Heat oven to 400°F. In 12-inch nonstick skillet, cook beef and onion over medium-high heat, stirring frequently, until beef is thoroughly cooked; drain. Stir in chili powder, salt and tomatoes. Remove from heat.

2 On ungreased large cookie sheet, unroll pie crusts. Spoon about 2 cups beef mixture onto half of each crust, spreading to within ½ inch of edge. Top each with ¼ cup cheese.

3 Brush edge of each crust with beaten egg. Fold untopped half of each crust over filling; press edge with fork to seal. Cut slits in several places in top of each; brush with beaten egg.

4 Bake 20 to 25 minutes or until golden brown. Cut into wedges to serve.

High Altitude (3500–6500 ft): No change.

1 Serving: Calories 510; Total Fat 31g (Saturated Fat 12g; Trans Fat 1g); Cholesterol 100mg; Sodium 690mg; Total Carbohydrate 39g (Dietary Fiber 2g) **Exchanges:** 2½ Starch, 2 Medium-Fat Meat, 4 Fat **Carbohydrate Choices:** 2½

Pie Tip If you like cilantro, chop 2 tablespoons, and add it to the empanada filling with the tomatoes.

country beef pot pie

Prep Time: 35 Minutes ✳ Start to Finish: 1 Hour 20 Minutes ✳ 6 servings

CRUST

1 box (15 oz) Pillsbury refrigerated pie crusts, softened as directed on box

FILLING

1 tablespoon vegetable oil

¾ lb boneless beef sirloin steak, cut into ½-inch cubes

1 medium onion, chopped (½ cup)

1 jar (12 oz) beef gravy

1 tablespoon cornstarch

2 teaspoons sugar

⅛ teaspoon pepper

2 cups frozen mixed vegetables

2 cups frozen southern-style diced hash brown potatoes (from 32-oz bag)

Sesame seed, if desired

1 Heat oven to 400°F. Make pie crusts as directed on package for Two-Crust Pie, using 9-inch glass pie plate.

2 In 10-inch skillet, heat oil over medium-high heat until hot. Add beef and onion; cook and stir until beef is browned. Drain.

3 In small bowl, mix gravy, cornstarch, sugar and pepper. Add to beef in skillet. Stir in vegetables and potatoes. Cook about 5 minutes, stirring occasionally, until vegetables are thawed. Spoon mixture into crust-lined pie plate. Top with second crust; seal edge and flute. Cut slits in several places in top crust. Sprinkle with sesame seed.

4 Bake 35 to 45 minutes or until golden brown. Let stand 10 minutes before serving.

High Altitude (3500–6500 ft): No change.

1 Serving: Calories 670; Total Fat 37g (Saturated Fat 12g; Trans Fat 2.5g); Cholesterol 40mg; Sodium 950mg; Total Carbohydrate 68g (Dietary Fiber 3g) **Exchanges:** 4 Starch, ½ Other Carbohydrate, 1 Lean Meat, 6 Fat **Carbohydrate Choices:** 4½

Pie Tip Bake the pie on a foil-lined cookie sheet; the foil catches drips and the cookie sheet makes it easy to move the pie plate in and out of the oven.

hot beef and mushroom turnovers

Prep Time: 15 Minutes ✳ Start to Finish: 30 Minutes ✳ 2 servings

CRUST

1 Pillsbury refrigerated pie crust (from 15-oz box), softened as directed on box

FILLING

4 thin slices deli roast beef (5 to 6 oz)

2 tablespoons steak sauce

4 slices Muenster cheese (1 oz)

SAUCE

½ cup beef gravy (from 12-oz jar)

1 jar (2.5 oz) sliced mushrooms, well drained

1 Heat oven to 425°F. Unroll pie crust on work surface. Cut crust in half. On ungreased cookie sheet, place crust halves.

2 On one side of each crust half, place half the roast beef, folding beef to fit. Top each with steak sauce and cheese. Fold crust over filling, pressing edges with fork to seal. Cut several slits in top of each.

3 Bake 13 to 18 minutes or until crust is deep golden brown. Meanwhile, in 1-quart saucepan, cook gravy and mushrooms over medium heat until hot. Serve sauce over turnovers.

High Altitude (3500–6500 ft): No change.

1 Serving: Calories 1220; Total Fat 78g (Saturated Fat 30g; Trans Fat 1g); Cholesterol 90mg; Sodium 1640mg; Total Carbohydrate 110g (Dietary Fiber 1g) **Exchanges:** 3½ Starch, ½ Fruit, 3½ Other Carbohydrate, 1 Lean Meat, 14 Fat **Carbohydrate Choices:** 7

Pie Tip You can easily make 4 turnovers by using both crusts in the box and doubling the other ingredients. This is a great recipe to use leftover beef roast and gravy.

barbecue pork pot pie

Prep Time: 20 Minutes ❋ Start to Finish: 1 Hour 5 Minutes ❋ 6 servings

CRUST

1 Pillsbury refrigerated pie crust (from 15-oz box), softened as directed on box

FILLING

1 container (18 oz) refrigerated original BBQ sauce with shredded pork

1½ cups frozen southern-style diced hash brown potatoes (from 32-oz bag)

1½ cups frozen whole kernel corn, thawed, drained

1½ cups shredded Cheddar cheese (6 oz)

1 Heat oven to 425°F. Place pie crust in 9-inch glass pie plate as directed on box for One-Crust Baked Shell; flute edge. Bake 5 to 7 minutes or until very lightly browned.

2 Remove partially baked crust from oven. Spoon half of shredded pork into crust. Top with potatoes, thawed corn and half of the cheese. Spoon remaining shredded pork over top. Sprinkle with remaining cheese. Cover crust edge with foil to prevent excessive browning.

3 Return pie to oven; bake 30 to 35 minutes longer or until crust is golden brown and cheese is melted. Let stand 10 minutes before serving. Cut into wedges.

High Altitude (3500–6500 ft): No change.

1 Serving: Calories 650; Total Fat 31g (Saturated Fat 13g; Trans Fat 0g); Cholesterol 60mg; Sodium 890mg; Total Carbohydrate 72g (Dietary Fiber 2g) **Exchanges:** 2½ Starch, 2 Other Carbohydrate, 2 High-Fat Meat, 2½ Fat **Carbohydrate Choices:** 5

barbecue beef pot pie: Substitute 1 container (18 oz) refrigerated shredded beef in original barbecue sauce for the shredded pork.

Pie Tip Southern-style hash brown potatoes are cubed; country-style hash browns are shredded. This recipe calls for the southern-style, but both styles work well.

pork picadillo pie

Prep Time: 30 Minutes ✳ Start to Finish: 1 Hour 15 Minutes ✳ 6 servings

CRUST

1 box (15 oz) Pillsbury refrigerated pie crusts, softened as directed on box

FILLING

1 lb boneless pork loin, cut into ½-inch cubes

½ cup chopped onion (1 medium)

1 can (14.5 oz) diced tomatoes, undrained

1 box (9 oz) frozen whole kernel corn

1 can (4.5 oz) chopped green chiles

½ cup chili sauce or ketchup

¼ cup sliced pimiento-stuffed green olives

¼ cup raisins

½ teaspoon ground cumin

¼ teaspoon salt

2 teaspoons milk

1 tablespoon cornmeal

1 Heat oven to 425°F. Make pie crusts as directed on box for Two-Crust Pie, using 9½- or 10-inch deep-dish glass pie plate.

2 Spray 12-inch skillet with cooking spray; heat over medium-high heat until hot. Add pork and onion; cook 3 to 5 minutes, stirring occasionally, until pork is no longer pink.

3 Add tomatoes, corn, green chiles, chili sauce, olives, raisins, cumin and salt. Heat to boiling. Reduce heat to medium; simmer 5 minutes, stirring occasionally, until slightly thickened. Remove from heat; cool 5 minutes.

4 Spoon mixture into crust-lined pie plate. Cut 4 wide slits or small designs in second crust; place crust over pork mixture. Seal edges and flute. Brush with milk; sprinkle with cornmeal.

5 Bake 25 to 35 minutes or until deep golden brown. Cover crust edge with foil after 10 to 15 minutes of baking to prevent excessive browning. Let pie stand 5 to 10 minutes before serving.

High Altitude (3500–6500 ft): In step 3, add 1 tablespoon all-purpose flour with the other ingredients.

1 Serving: Calories 550; Total Fat 26g (Saturated Fat 9g; Trans Fat 0g); Cholesterol 60mg; Sodium 1240mg; Total Carbohydrate 59g (Dietary Fiber 4g) **Exchanges:** 2½ Starch, 1 Other Carbohydrate, 1 Vegetable, 1½ Lean Meat, 4 Fat **Carbohydrate Choices:** 4

Pie Tip Cumin is the tiny dried fruit of a plant in the parsley family and is often used in Mexican dishes. It's very aromatic and has a pungent nutty flavor.

ham and broccoli quiche

Prep Time: 15 Minutes ✳ Start to Finish: 1 Hour 5 Minutes ✳ 6 servings

CRUST

1 Pillsbury refrigerated pie crust (from 15-oz box), softened as directed on box

FILLING

1½ cups cubed cooked ham

1½ cups shredded Swiss cheese (6 oz)

1 cup frozen broccoli florets, thawed, well drained

4 eggs

1 cup milk

½ teaspoon salt

½ teaspoon ground mustard

½ teaspoon pepper

1 Heat oven to 375°F. Make pie crust as directed on box for One-Crust Filled Pie, using 9-inch glass pie plate.

2 Layer ham, cheese and thawed broccoli in crust-lined pie plate. In medium bowl, beat remaining filling ingredients with a whisk until well blended. Pour over broccoli.

3 Bake 35 to 45 minutes or until knife inserted in center comes out clean. Let stand 5 minutes before serving. Cut into wedges.

High Altitude (3500–6500 ft): In step 3, bake 45 to 55 minutes; during last 15 minutes of baking, cover crust edge with strips of foil to prevent excessive browning.

1 Serving: Calories 560; Total Fat 36g (Saturated Fat 15g; Trans Fat 0g); Cholesterol 200mg; Sodium 920mg; Total Carbohydrate 40g (Dietary Fiber 0g) **Exchanges:** 2½ Starch, 2½ High-Fat Meat, 2½ Fat **Carbohydrate Choices:** 2½

turkey and broccoli quiche: Substitute 1½ cups cubed cooked turkey or chicken for the ham.

Pie Tip If there are larger pieces of broccoli, cut them into smaller ones so the florets are of uniform size and will cook evenly.

sausage and roasted pepper calzone

Tony DeSantis | Port Blanchard, PA | Bake-Off® Contest 34, 1990

Pillsbury Bake-Off

Prep Time: 30 Minutes ❋ Start to Finish: 55 Minutes ❋ 6 servings

FILLING

1 lb bulk sweet Italian sausage

½ cup sliced green onions (8 medium)

1 clove garlic, finely chopped

¼ teaspoon dried basil leaves

¼ teaspoon Italian seasoning

¼ teaspoon pepper

2 eggs

⅓ cup ricotta cheese

8 oz mozzarella cheese, cut into ¼-inch cubes (2 cups)

1 jar (7 oz) roasted red bell peppers, drained, chopped

¼ cup pine nuts

CRUST

1 box (15 oz) Pillsbury refrigerated pie crusts, softened as directed on box

1 Heat oven to 400°F. Meanwhile, in 10-inch nonstick skillet, mix sausage, onions and garlic; cook and stir over medium-high heat 5 to 7 minutes or until sausage is no longer pink; drain. Stir in basil, Italian seasoning and pepper.

2 In small bowl, beat eggs. Measure out and reserve 1½ tablespoons egg. Add ricotta cheese to remaining eggs; mix well. Stir into sausage mixture. Add mozzarella cheese, roasted peppers and 3 tablespoons of the pine nuts; mix well.

3 Unroll 1 pie crust on end of large ungreased cookie sheet with about ⅓ of crust extending over edge. Spoon half of sausage mixture over half of crust on cookie sheet, leaving about 1-inch border and mounding filling toward center. Fold pie crust half over filling; press edges with fork to seal. Cut four 1-inch slits in top of crust. Repeat with second crust and remaining filling at opposite end of cookie sheet. Brush calzones with reserved 1½ tablespoons egg. Sprinkle with remaining pine nuts.

4 Bake 20 to 25 minutes or until crust is golden brown. To serve, cut each calzone into 3 wedges.

High Altitude (3500–6500 ft): In step 4, bake 25 to 30 minutes.

1 Serving: Calories 700; Total Fat 48g (Saturated Fat 18g; Trans Fat 0g); Cholesterol 135mg; Sodium 1200mg; Total Carbohydrate 43g (Dietary Fiber 1g) **Exchanges:** 2½ Other Carbohydrate, ½ Vegetable, 1½ Medium-Fat Meat, 2 High-Fat Meat, 5 Fat **Carbohydrate Choices:** 3

empanada grande

Prep Time: 15 Minutes ✳ Start to Finish: 45 Minutes ✳ 3 servings

CRUST

1 Pillsbury refrigerated pie crust (from 15-oz box), softened as directed on box

FILLING

1 egg

4 oz smoked chorizo sausage links or kielbasa, casing removed, coarsely chopped (about 1 cup)

¾ cup frozen shredded hash brown potatoes (from 30-oz bag), thawed

⅓ cup frozen sweet peas

1 small onion, chopped (¼ cup)

¼ teaspoon salt

1 Heat oven to 400°F. On ungreased large cookie sheet, unroll pie crust.

2 In large bowl, beat egg thoroughly with whisk. Reserve 1 tablespoon egg in small bowl. Stir remaining filling ingredients into egg in large bowl.

3 Spoon filling mixture evenly onto half of crust to within ½ inch of edge. Brush edge of crust with reserved 1 tablespoon beaten egg. Fold crust over filling; press edges with fork to seal. Cut several slits in top of crust. Brush top with remaining beaten egg.

4 Bake 25 to 30 minutes or until golden brown. Cut into wedges.

High Altitude (3500–6500 ft): Thaw frozen peas before use.

1 Serving: Calories 560; Total Fat 35g (Saturated Fat 13g; Trans Fat 0g); Cholesterol 115mg; Sodium 1000mg; Total Carbohydrate 49g (Dietary Fiber 2g) **Exchanges:** 3 Starch, ½ High-Fat Meat, 6 Fat **Carbohydrate Choices:** 3

Pie Tip If you forgot to thaw the potatoes, you can quickly thaw them in the microwave. Place them on a microwavable plate, and microwave uncovered on Medium for 1 minute.

crab, broccoli and roasted red pepper quiche

Prep Time: 35 Minutes ✳ Start to Finish: 1 Hour 35 Minutes ✳ 6 servings

CRUST

1 Pillsbury refrigerated pie crust (from 15-oz box), softened as directed on box

FILLING

1 can (6 oz) white crabmeat, well drained

1 cup frozen cut broccoli, thawed, drained well on paper towel

1 cup shredded provolone cheese (4 oz)

⅓ cup chopped roasted red bell peppers (from a jar), well drained

2 tablespoons shredded fresh Parmesan cheese

4 eggs

1 cup milk

¼ teaspoon salt

⅛ teaspoon ground red pepper (cayenne)

1 Heat oven to 425°F. Bake pie crust as directed on box for One-Crust Baked Shell, using 9-inch glass pie plate.

2 Remove baked crust form oven. Reduce oven temperature to 350°F. Layer crabmeat, broccoli, provolone cheese, roasted peppers and Parmesan cheese in baked crust.

3 In medium bowl, beat eggs with whisk until well blended. Add milk, salt and ground red pepper; blend well. Pour over mixture in crust. Cover crust edge with foil to prevent excessive browning.

4 Bake 50 to 60 minutes or until knife inserted in center comes out clean. Let stand 5 to 10 minutes before serving.

High Altitude (3500–6500 ft): No change.

1 Serving: Calories 480; Total Fat 29g (Saturated Fat 12g; Trans Fat 0g); Cholesterol 190mg; Sodium 730mg; Total Carbohydrate 39g (Dietary Fiber 1g) **Exchanges:** 2½ Starch, 1 Medium-Fat Meat, 4½ Fat **Carbohydrate Choices:** 2½

 Choose the best quality canned crabmeat, such as that labeled "fancy" for best results. If you like, use 1 cup fresh or frozen crabmeat, thawed, drained and flaked, instead of the canned crabmeat.

tuna empanadas

Prep Time: 35 Minutes ✳ Start to Finish: 55 Minutes ✳ 10 empanadas

FILLING

2 teaspoons olive oil

¼ cup finely chopped onion

1 teaspoon finely chopped garlic

½ cup canned diced tomatoes, undrained

⅓ cup tomato sauce

1 pouch (3 oz) albacore tuna in water

¼ cup quartered green olives stuffed with pimiento

½ teaspoon salt

1 tablespoon chopped fresh parsley

1 tablespoon finely chopped fresh cilantro

1 bay leaf

1 canned chipotle chile in adobo sauce

1 tablespoon sauce from canned chipotle chiles in adobo sauce

CRUST

1 box (15 oz) Pillsbury refrigerated pie crusts, softened as directed on box

1 Heat oven to 350°F. In 12-inch skillet, heat oil over medium-high heat until hot. Cook onion and garlic in oil about 2 minutes, stirring occasionally, until onion is tender. Stir in tomatoes and tomato sauce. Cook until tomatoes are soft, stirring occasionally. Stir in remaining filling ingredients. Cook until mixture thickens, stirring occasionally. Remove from heat; remove bay leaf.

2 On lightly floured surface, unroll 1 pie crust. With rolling pin, roll crust into 14-inch round. Using 4½-inch round cutter, cut 5 rounds. Repeat with second crust. Spoon 1 rounded tablespoonful filling onto half of each round. Moisten edge of each round with water. Fold in half; press edge with fork to seal. On ungreased cookie sheet, place empanadas 2 inches apart. Poke top of each once with fork to vent steam.

3 Bake about 20 minutes or until light golden brown. Loosely cover and refrigerate any remaining empanadas.

High Altitude (3500–6500 ft): No change.

1 Empanada: Calories 170; Total Fat 10g (Saturated Fat 3g; Trans Fat 0g); Cholesterol 5mg; Sodium 420mg; Total Carbohydrate 18g (Dietary Fiber 0g) **Exchanges:** 1 Starch, 2 Fat **Carbohydrate Choices:** 1

Pie Tip For golden brown empanadas, brush with egg wash before baking. To make the egg wash, beat 1 egg and 1 tablespoon water until well mixed.

three-pepper galette

Prep Time: 15 Minutes ✳ Start to Finish: 50 Minutes ✳ 6 servings

CRUST

1 Pillsbury refrigerated pie crust (from 15-oz box), softened as directed on box

FILLING

¼ medium green bell pepper, cut into 2×¼-inch strips (about ½ cup)

¼ medium red bell pepper, cut into 2×¼-inch strips (about ½ cup)

¼ medium yellow bell pepper, cut into 2×¼-inch strips (about ½ cup)

⅓ cup milk

2 eggs

1 container (4 oz) garlic-and-herbs spreadable cheese

¼ cup shredded Italian cheese blend

1 Heat oven to 400°F. Place pie crust in 9-inch glass pie plate as directed on box for One-Crust Filled Pie. Arrange half of the peppers in crust-lined pie plate (see photo).

2 In small bowl, beat milk, eggs and spreadable cheese with electric mixer on low speed until well blended. Pour over peppers in pie plate. Arrange remaining peppers on top of egg mixture. Fold edge of crust over filling, pleating crust slightly as needed.

3 Bake 20 to 30 minutes or until crust is golden brown and center is set. Sprinkle with cheese blend. Bake 3 to 5 minutes longer or until cheese is melted. Sprinkle with basil. Serve immediately.

High Altitude (3500–6500 ft): In step 3, increase first bake time to 25 to 30 minutes.

1 Serving: Calories 280; Total Fat 12g (Saturated Fat 6g; Trans Fat 0g); Cholesterol 95mg; Sodium 590mg; Total Carbohydrate 33g (Dietary Fiber 0g) **Exchanges:** 1 Starch, 1 Other Carbohydrate, 1 Medium-Fat Meat, 1½ Fat **Carbohydrate Choices:** 2

Pie Tip A variety of bell peppers adds color to this galette, but you can use just one color if you like. For a spicier pie, add a chopped jalapeño chile to the filling.

Pleating Crust

Fold edge of crust over filling, pleating crust slightly as needed to fit.

vegetable-cheddar quiche

Prep Time: 25 Minutes ✳ Start to Finish: 1 Hour 10 Minutes ✳ 6 servings

CRUST
1 Pillsbury refrigerated pie crust (from 15-oz box), softened as directed on box

FILLING
1½ cups shredded Cheddar cheese (6 oz)

2 tablespoons all-purpose flour

2 cups frozen bell pepper and onion stir-fry (from 1-lb bag), thawed, drained and patted dry

1 can (4 oz) mushroom pieces and stems, drained

4 eggs

1 cup milk

¼ teaspoon salt

⅛ teaspoon pepper

1 Heat oven to 425°F. Place pie crust in 9-inch glass pie plate or quiche dish as directed on box for One-Crust Filled Pie. Bake 5 to 7 minutes or just until edge begins to brown. If crust puffs up in center, gently push down with back of wooden spoon.

2 Meanwhile, in large bowl, mix cheese and flour; toss to coat. Add bell pepper and onion stir-fry, and mushrooms; toss to mix.

3 Remove partially baked crust from oven; reduce oven temperature to 375°F. Spoon cheese mixture into crust. In same bowl, mix remaining ingredients; beat until well blended. Pour over cheese mixture.

4 Bake at 375°F 35 to 45 minutes or until filling is puffed and knife inserted in center comes out clean. If necessary, cover crust edge with foil during last 15 to 20 minutes of baking to prevent excessive browning. Let stand 5 to 10 minutes before serving.

High Altitude (3500–6500 ft): No change.

1 Serving: Calories 520; Total Fat 33g (Saturated Fat 14g; Trans Fat 0g); Cholesterol 185mg; Sodium 670mg; Total Carbohydrate 44g (Dietary Fiber 1g) **Exchanges:** 3 Starch, 1 High-Fat Meat, 4 Fat **Carbohydrate Choices:** 3

 Frozen bell pepper and onion stir-fry is a versatile mixture of red, yellow and green bell peppers plus onions. The mixture thaws quickly in the microwave using half the time recommended in the package cooking directions. Or to thaw even more quickly, place the veggies in a strainer and run warm water over them until thawed.

leek quiche

Prep Time: 25 Minutes ✳ Start to Finish: 1 Hour 15 Minutes ✳ 6 servings

CRUST

1 Pillsbury refrigerated pie
crust (from 15-oz box),
softened as directed on box

FILLING

2 medium leeks

2 tablespoons butter or
margarine

3 eggs

1 cup milk

1 cup shredded Swiss cheese
(4 oz)

½ teaspoon salt

¼ teaspoon pepper

⅛ teaspoon ground nutmeg

1 Heat oven to 400°F. Place pie crust in 9-inch glass pie plate as directed on box for One-Crust Filled Pie. Bake about 8 minutes or until very lightly browned.

2 Meanwhile, wash leeks; remove any tough outer leaves. Trim roots from white bulb portion. Cut leeks lengthwise and wash well. Cut crosswise into ½-inch-thick slices to make about 4 cups; set aside.

3 In 12-inch skillet, melt butter over medium heat. Add leeks; cook 7 to 9 minutes, stirring frequently, until tender but not brown. Remove from heat; set aside.

4 In small bowl, beat eggs with whisk. Stir in remaining filling ingredients until blended. Stir in cooked leeks. Pour mixture into partially baked crust.

5 Bake quiche 10 minutes. Cover crust edge with foil to prevent excessive browning. Reduce oven temperature to 300°F. Bake 20 to 25 minutes or until knife inserted in center comes out clean. Cool 15 minutes before serving.

High Altitude (3500–6500 ft): In step 5, after covering crust edge with foil, reduce oven temperature to 350°F. Bake 25 to 30 minutes.

1 Serving: Calories 340; Total Fat 22g (Saturated Fat 10g; Trans Fat 1g); Cholesterol 140mg; Sodium 470mg; Total Carbohydrate 24g (Dietary Fiber 0g) **Exchanges:** 1½ Starch, 1 High-Fat Meat, 2½ Fat **Carbohydrate Choices:** 1½

Pie Tip Leeks look like giant green onions and are related to both onions and garlic. Choose leeks that are firm and bright colored with an unblemished white bulb portion. Smaller leeks will be more tender than larger ones. Be sure to wash leeks thoroughly because there is often sand between the layers.

provolone and pesto quiche

Prep Time: 15 Minutes ✳ Start to Finish: 1 Hour 10 Minutes ✳ 8 servings

CRUST

1 Pillsbury refrigerated pie crust (from 15-oz box), softened as directed on box

FILLING

2 cups shredded Provolone cheese (8 oz)

3 tablespoons refrigerated basil pesto

¼ cup grated Parmesan cheese

½ cup chopped red bell pepper

5 eggs

1½ cups milk

¼ teaspoon salt

1 Heat oven to 425°F. Place pie crust in 9-inch glass pie plate as directed on box for One-Crust Filled Pie. Bake 7 minutes.

2 Remove crust from oven. Sprinkle 1 cup of the Provolone cheese over bottom of crust.

3 In small bowl, mix pesto and Parmesan cheese until smooth. Carefully spread over Provolone cheese. Sprinkle with bell pepper and remaining Provolone cheese.

4 In large bowl, beat eggs, milk and salt with whisk until well blended. Pour over cheese.

5 Bake 7 minutes. Reduce oven temperature to 325°F. Bake 15 minutes. Cover crust edge with foil to prevent excessive browning. Bake 23 to 28 minutes longer or until set and knife inserted in center comes out clean. Let stand 5 minutes before serving.

High Altitude (3500–6500 ft): No change.

1 Serving: Calories 330; Total Fat 23g (Saturated Fat 10g; Trans Fat 0g); Cholesterol 165mg; Sodium 590mg; Total Carbohydrate 17g (Dietary Fiber 0g) **Exchanges:** ½ Starch, ½ Other Carbohydrate, 2 High-Fat Meat, 1½ Fat **Carbohydrate Choices:** 1

 Baking the crust slightly before adding the filling helps ensure that the crust bakes thoroughly and will be flaky and not soggy.

quesadilla quiche

Laurie Keane | Escondido, CA | Bake-Off® Contest 33, 1988

Prep Time: 25 Minutes ✳ Start to Finish: 1 Hour 25 Minutes ✳ 6 servings

CRUST

1 box (15 oz) Pillsbury refrigerated pie crusts, softened as directed on box

FILLING

1 tablespoon butter or margarine

1 cup coarsely chopped onions

1 cup coarsely chopped tomato, drained

1 can (3.8 oz) sliced ripe olives, drained

¼ teaspoon garlic powder or garlic salt

¼ teaspoon ground cumin

⅛ teaspoon pepper

1 can (4.5 oz) chopped green chiles, drained

2 eggs, beaten

2 to 3 drops red pepper sauce

1 cup shredded Monterey Jack cheese (4 oz)

1 cup shredded Cheddar cheese (4 oz)

SERVE WITH

Sour cream, if desired

Chunky-style salsa or picante, if desired

1 Make pie crust as directed on box for Two-Crust Pie, using 10-inch tart pan with removable bottom or 9-inch glass pie plate. Place 1 pie crust in pan; press in bottom and up side. Trim edges if necessary.

2 Move oven rack to lowest position; heat oven to 375°F. In 8-inch skillet, melt butter over medium heat. Cook and stir onions in butter until tender. Reserve 1 tablespoon each chopped tomato and ripe olives. Stir remaining tomato and olives, the garlic powder, cumin, pepper and chiles into cooked onion.

3 In small bowl, beat eggs and red pepper sauce with fork. Reserve 2 teaspoons mixture. Stir in ½ cup of the Monterey Jack cheese and ½ cup of the Cheddar cheese. Sprinkle remaining cheeses in bottom of crust-lined pan. Spoon onion mixture evenly over cheese. Carefully pour egg mixture over onion mixture; spread to cover.

4 Top with second crust; seal edges. Cut slits in top crust in several places. Brush with reserved egg mixture.

5 Place pan on lowest oven rack. Bake 45 to 55 minutes or until golden brown. Let stand 5 minutes; remove sides of pan. To remove tart from sides of pan, place the pan on a wide, short can and pull down the side of the pan (see page 80). If necessary, use a thin-bladed knife to loosen crust from the side of the pan. Serve warm with sour cream, salsa and reserved chopped tomatoes and olives.

High Altitude (3500–6500 ft): In step 5, bake 50 to 55 minutes.

1 Serving: Calories 540; Total Fat 36g (Saturated Fat 16g; Trans Fat 0g); Cholesterol 120mg; Sodium 1010mg; Total Carbohydrate 41g (Dietary Fiber 2g) **Exchanges:** 2½ Starch, ½ Other Carbohydrate, ½ High-Fat Meat, 6 Fat **Carbohydrate Choices:** 3

Metric Conversion Guide

Volume

U.S. UNITS	CANADIAN METRIC	AUSTRALIAN METRIC
¼ teaspoon	1 mL	1 ml
½ teaspoon	2 mL	2 ml
1 teaspoon	5 mL	5 ml
1 tablespoon	15 mL	20 ml
¼ cup	50 mL	60 ml
⅓ cup	75 mL	80 ml
½ cup	125 mL	125 ml
⅔ cup	150 mL	170 ml
¾ cup	175 mL	190 ml
1 cup	250 mL	250 ml
1 quart	1 liter	1 liter
1½ quarts	1.5 liters	1.5 liters
2 quarts	2 liters	2 liters
2½ quarts	2.5 liters	2.5 liters
3 quarts	3 liters	3 liters
4 quarts	4 liters	4 liters

Weight

U.S. UNITS	CANADIAN METRIC	AUSTRALIAN METRIC
1 ounce	30 grams	30 grams
2 ounces	55 grams	60 grams
3 ounces	85 grams	90 grams
4 ounces (¼ pound)	115 grams	125 grams
8 ounces (½ pound)	225 grams	225 grams
16 ounces (1 pound)	455 grams	500 grams
1 pound	455 grams	0.5 kilogram

Measurements

INCHES	CENTIMETERS
1	2.5
2	5.0
3	7.5
4	10.0
5	12.5
6	15.0
7	17.5
8	20.5
9	23.0
10	25.5
11	28.0
12	30.5
13	33.0

Temperatures

FAHRENHEIT	CELSIUS
32°	0°
212°	100°
250°	120°
275°	140°
300°	150°
325°	160°
350°	180°
375°	190°
400°	200°
425°	220°
450°	230°
475°	240°
500°	260°

NOTE: The recipes in this cookbook have not been developed or tested using metric measures. When converting recipes to metric, some variations in quality may be noted.

Index

Page numbers in *italics* indicate illustrations.

Notes on Recipe Testing and Calculating Nutrition

Recipe Testing:

- Large eggs and 2% milk were used unless otherwise indicated.

- Fat-free, low-fat, low-sodium or lite products were not used unless indicated.

- No nonstick cookware and bakeware were used unless otherwise indicated. No dark-colored, black or insulated bakeware was used.

- When a pan is specified, a metal pan was used; a baking dish or pie plate means ovenproof glass was used.

- An electric hand mixer was used for mixing only when mixer speeds are specified.

Calculating Nutrition:

- The first ingredient was used wherever a choice is given, such as $\frac{1}{3}$ cup sour cream or plain yogurt.

- The first amount was used wherever a range is given, such as 3- to $3\frac{1}{2}$-pound whole chicken.

- The first serving number was used wherever a range is given, such as 4 to 6 servings.

- "If desired" ingredients were not included.

- Only the amount of a marinade or frying oil that is absorbed was included.

Hungry for more?
See what else
Pillsbury has to offer.

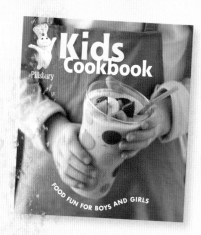